SQUARE PEG ROUND HOLE

A Family's survival of Developmental Dispraxia and Dyslexia.

K.E.Pickard

authorHOUSE®

AuthorHouse™ UK Ltd.
500 Avebury Boulevard
Central Milton Keynes, MK9 2BE
www.authorhouse.co.uk
Phone: 08001974150

First published by AuthorHouse 5/5/2011

ISBN: 978-1-4567-7996-2 (sc)
ISBN: 978-1-4567-7997-9 (e)

Library of Congress Control Number: 2011907206

Certain stock imagery © Thinkstock.

This book is printed on acid-free paper.

CONTENTS

PREVIEW

The writing of this book is intended to help any parent, family member, doctor, teacher etc. To give an insight into the difficulties experienced by a child of specific learning difficulties and to highlight the difficulties one family faced whilst trying to help their child.

My intention is to show that what we think is necessary is not always the way forward; the education authority and parents alike need to listen more carefully to the child's voice and we must not always think we as adults know what is best.

To be an individual and to be a free thinker has been the way of many of the worlds greatest men and women. Science relies on it, yet when it comes to our children we try to make all children fit into the same box. To read by the same age, to develop at the same pace. Whilst we must recognise that some guidelines must be in place we must also realise that all children are individuals and celebrate that.

This is a true account of a family from England who had a child and who later discovered that their child had specific learning difficulties. The journey the family took from the birth of that child to the 21st birthday. The school experience, the help that was or was not available. The highs and the lows of life. The despair of the child and the journey he took in order to conform to other peoples view points and teacher and doctors ideas of who he should be, how he should act and at what time in his life he should have developed certain skills.

This book is dedicated to my son who is the most wonderful and amazing human being whom I am sure will go on to do great things and have a very full and happy life.

All names and places have been withheld or changed in the writing of the book

PART 1

THE EARLY YEARS.

It was a blissful day when we found out we were pregnant. We were already the proud parents of two wonderful boys both of whom were school age and who went to the local junior school. They were very happy boys who loved to play out, loved bikes and most of all loved each other. They were and I hate to use this word, simply normal, although I realise that word is relative. We both worked and in fact we both had very good secure jobs. We lived in a small village and owned our own home. Both boys had their own bedrooms and like most children possibly had too much in the way of toys etc. In our village lived both sets of grandparents so the family unit was ideal from any perspective. A third child for us at this time was quite simply wonderful news.

The pregnancy was easy, I was very well and I worked right up to just before the birth. As things were ideal we opted to have the child at a local cottage hospital not five miles away. Our family GP would be available to deliver the baby and being my third pregnancy nothing worried me at all. I am 5feet 1inches tall and I was at this time 27 years old. I was huge to look at but I normally have a very slight build and was in fact at the time of delivery exactly 8 stone . Now I know some people will be shocked at this but as I said this is normal for me I had in fact put on a very acceptable ten pounds, all baby I might add. So once again everything was ideal.

As I started in labour I knew this baby would be a boy as it was late and both my other sons were late, simply I think boys just become far to comfortable. I did not rush to the hospital as third labour tells you that this is going to take a long time. My mother arrived to look after the boys early in the morning and take them to school and we went quietly on our journey to the hospital.

We were very excited we love our children and the new arrival was long awaited. The drive to the hospital was uneventful and beautiful as the hospital is set in its own country grounds amongst lots of tall trees. The month is early January and all the leaves have that lovely red and brown and golden quality. The midwife met us at the entrance of the hospital and I liked her very much. She was middle aged and talked to me about how many children she had delivered at this hospital in her years. Significant for her, as this hospital was facing closure due to health budgets and I can tell you it closed soon after. It was all very relaxed indeed, very different from a larger hospital. The midwife placed a call to the doctor who was five minutes away and after she examined me she said that the baby was very near. They did offer me pain killers which I said I did not need as the delivery would be quite quick. The doctor came and examined me and said it would not be long. I was pushing and they advised me to try to wait a while, so as you do, I tried. The doctor looked again and said the baby was not quite ready, he would go for his sandwich but be close at hand. Now, I was in agony so I asked for pain killers which they said I now could not have as the baby was so close. When the doctor left I cried and said to the midwife something is wrong the baby will not come. My husband tried to humour me, as they can only do in this situation, but I told him to stand by me and make them do something. At this point the older midwife looked at me and said she could help me if I would let her, my answer was do anything as I fear the baby is stuck. She asked me to trust her and her experience and I did, she obviously knew her stuff. I do not know exactly what she did, some how she helped the baby and seconds later sat upright on the bed was the biggest baby I have ever seen. He was chubby and resembled the little Michelin baby we have all seen on the front of the wagons. His head was huge, and just like our other children he was very blonde and absolutely beautiful. My husband looked on adoringly and he was the first after the midwife to hold our son. I looked on as he walked around the room talking to him softly. The doctor came back to the room at this point and they began to check his fingers and toes and weigh and measure him. The midwife called out the weight and the doctor asked that it be checked again. Our son was a whopping 10'pounds 9'ounces and his head circumference was very large. The fish tank they placed him in was only just a fit. Our son went softly to sleep and I basked in a lovely bubble bath. I asked if I could go home now and they asked me to please stay just one night and then I could go early the next morning. I reluctantly agreed as I simply wanted to be with my family, and as I declared I was in fact starving so they made me reams of baked beans on toast. It was the best I ever tasted. On the ward were two other mothers who had previously given birth to dainty little girls. They were lovely, I looked on lovingly to my son and I saw just how cuddly he was, I mean chubby and extremely cute. The night was uneventful and in the early morning of the next day my husband came to get us.

We arrived home shortly afterwards to a lovely welcome of nearly the whole family and then the whole village. Everyone marvelled at him as most babies resemble sort of skinned rabbits -pardon the phrase- but our son was lovely looking like a eight week old baby instead of a brand new one. I breast fed and over the next few days the midwife's came and went checking all was all right which of course it was. I was taking a five year career break with my son which meant I could be on hand to take my sons to school , collect them at the end of the day and enjoy our new son until after he had started school. Our sons were 8, 6 and newborn respectfully.

Life was tranquil. The boys loved their new brother and went to school happily every morning. Our new born slept, woke to eat and by the time I changed his nappy he was asleep again I kid you not. He slept and slept happily feeding as often as he could, gurgling and then sleeping some more. All my friends with new children stared in envy at my huge but sleeping son. Now at the time of the check ups at the baby clinic I learned that my son was above the top percentile when he was born and as he grew he continued to be above the top percentile. For those who don't know what this is, the medical profession have three simple wavy lines which represent most of the population. The lower line being for the shorter smaller people like me, the middle line is for well obviously the middle size people and the top line for the taller larger people. When a mother takes a child to baby clinic and then later to the doctors etc they weigh and measure the child as it develops and place a small star on a graph which shows the development and growth of that child. Well my son was above and I mean above the top line, at the age of four months I was no longer breast feeding as this was not enough I was bottle feeding and yes I admit it I was also giving him small amounts of baby rice. This is against all the rules as far as feeding baby is concerned it was deemed far too early, but look this was my third child and he was quite simply starving. So I fed him more and more and he just grew and grew, I kid you not at the age of 9months he looked like an eighteen month old baby. When he was one year old he looked two and so on. I am sure you get the general idea. A very caring lady at the baby clinic did suggest, as they do these days that he was maybe a little fat. I admit again to saying OK I will take that under advisement but when I went home I looked at this huge lovely child and shrugged my shoulders and fed him more.

As he grew he preferred to eat rather than have milk, I made all my own baby food by simply mashing our veg and potatoes and he loved it. He hated sweet food but loved an occasional piece of fruit which he sucked to death and later munched away. He was a very very happy and content child, he hardly ever cried and loved everyone. As he developed I used to prop him up with cushions. He would sit, play and was happy. He never had a dummy of any kind, he did not need it.

I was in fact a very relaxed mother, this was my third child. Look in any playground and we can see that all children are different developing at different rates. When my child did not crawl at the allotted month I did not give it a second thought, nor did I care that he did not sit at the correct time or walk he was a big tall boy and I knew he would do these things in his own good time.

My son loved his brothers who talked to him constantly. They told him stories included him at all times even choosing to lie on the floor next to him whilst doing their homework. As they learned new skills so did he when he talked it was full intelligent sentences none of your baby talk here. When he could walk about he followed them everywhere looking and listening. At the age of eighteen months his party piece was counting to ten in French. He had learnt this parrot fashion from his brothers. At one baby clinic visit he was to have a developmental test and during this test he was asked to say what a duck was when a card was held in front of him, a ball and a car. He correctly said the words and as he sat on my knee the doctor marvelled as he counted to ten in French for her. He was given a very small bead on the desk and he was asked to pick it up, he looked at the doctor and did nothing. She repeated her request for him to pick up the bead, he used both hands and rolled the bead to the edge of the desk and slid the bead into his other palm. The doctor frustrated placed the bead down again and asked him to pick it up using his forefinger and thumb but he looked at her like she was silly and rolled the bead to the edge of the table and pushed it into his other palm.

I was later to find out the significance of this test but the doctor looked at him and smiled and said we will see him again in eight weeks. Eight weeks later as the doctor placed the bead on the desk a third time my son talked to her in French, talked about engines and his favourite subject of the time tractors. He was obviously very bright and even though he never picked the bead up with forefinger and thumb, as she listened to him talk on about his tractors she smiled and said no problems here then and he miraculously had passed a test he had actually failed. I was not in the least worried as my very bright son I thought had other things on his mind.

My son was also quite clumsy but I actually put this down to him being so tall and big, I prefer to think of him as a little awkward and and thought he would like a race horse sort of even out eventually and all things come together. He was happy, bubbly, and played and talked with us all constantly. His favourite television programme was not play school as I would have liked but a tape of the film "The Italian Job", he could recite the whole film at three, word for every word. He watched it every day sat on my husbands knee or sat with his brothers and even sat alone. His brothers and his father have a fascination for cars and the baby was no exception.

NURSERY SCHOOL.

In our small village we as villagers had always felt very privileged, the reason was we had our very own council owned Nursery school which offered priority places to village children. This was fantastic even when my husband and I were young, as it gives at three and a half years old a place at nursery school in the mornings or afternoons free of charge. The nursery school of course now was a small purpose built building and was slightly attached to the junior school the children would eventually move on to. This I thought was a fantastic idea. For our youngest son who was so bright, (do not misunderstand me all our children were very clever), we were very lucky indeed. Our youngest son was just very different. He was so interested in everything, and I mean everything. He loved books and had some member of the family or other person read to him all the time. Our older children were fanatical about Lego and Play mobile and made worlds with pirate ships and Star wars space ships, including our youngest all the time. Then as our baby reached the age of three years I was allowed to choose a slot at the local nursery school if we wished and of course I thought it had arrived at the best time as I was trying to fill his day with art play, nature walks, stories, and collecting started of insects and bugs and he had developed a strong interest in dinosaurs. This was I thought like most boys of a young age although his interest was very strong indeed.

I chose mornings sessions at the nursery school because he still ate and slept for hours at a time, after any lunch he would sleep for three hours minimum. So I decided after a hard mornings play at school he could still take his long nap. Ideal for any mother, since his birth I had enjoyed his company as he was a very interesting little person with no malice in him at all for anything or anyone, he chatted constantly and laughed and joked all the time. Now I am sure all parents will say the same about their children but he was very interesting company and a complete joy to be around. Very good for me as I found I had no time for children who sulked constantly, or who spoke in baby talk annoyingly pointing to the things they wanted. Our days started very early at seven in the morning, my other sons would eat breakfast, chat about their forthcoming day and eventually we would all set off to school, the epic journey of about 4oo yards. Then having seen the boys safely into the gates we would head back home and my son would chat to me whilst I dashed around cleaning and tidying for about a half an hour. My son would beam at me as he knew from routine that our time had come and we would eagerly plan our day. This would include a walk, reading, collecting, museums, art, baking and many discussions about insects and dinosaurs and he would talk about tractors enjoying listing the different types, makes etc.

As you can see I was of the opinion that nursery school at three and a half years could simply not come soon enough for this young inquisitive mind. I would lie at night thinking about how he was going to enjoy so much learning even more than I could teach him. I was sure that trained professional teachers would find our son an absolute joy, how could they fail to, and in turn our son would soak up any and all information they could impart to him, fantastic.

The first morning came and we arrived at the school at 10 am together, I stayed much to my sons annoyance as he just simply wanted to get on with it and not have his mother around. He looked superb in his little school clothes and we were introduced to the handful of children twelve in total that would make up the morning sessions. Five children came from our village and the rest from the surrounding villages. My first view of the other children was utter shock, you see compared to my son, they looked so young and small. At three and a half he was about the size of a five year old tall and stocky, but, without an ounce of fat on him. The other children were small, dainty, and shockingly so young looking. Some were not toilet trained and all of them clung in some way to there respective parent. Some hardly spoke and grunted pointing to what they wanted. But I was sure all would be fine as all children grow and develop at different rates, right!.

On the morning of the second day our son happily chatted as I helped him dress for his second big day, off we went hand in hand to the school. When I collected him the teacher called me to one side, she stated that he seemed unable to remember to follow her simple instructions. I looked at the teacher as if she was an alien, was she actually saying this about my son, not possible. But she was, well what instructions do you mean I gasped. We have the need for routine and rules she said, the first is that when we play with the water play, we all put on an apron. Oh yes of course I said as routine was my middle name. Well your son forgets this rule, always. Its early days yet I said, all this nursery school stuff is so new and different I will talk to him and I am sure all will be fine for the future.

I have to say at this point I thought the woman had a screw loose, I mean really how terrible was forgetting to put on an apron. Please, I did mention it to him, but come on, not really thinking this would be a future problem. I mean problems were when my eldest son struggled with long division, or, when the middle son fell head first out of a tree.

Anyway, the days followed each other and every day when I arrived at nursery school to collect him there was some problem or another, the woman was actually driving me crazy. I listened, empathized, and made the right ooo sounds in different places but the problems she had, I thought, to be stupid. She was however a trained professional so I really did try to listen and help her with the problems. The problems were simple and silly things; he did not remember his apron at wet play time, he did not remember his apron at sand play time, he repeatedly took the dolls pram up a small slope that he was asked not to do and he never sat still during story time. "Does he run around" I asked ? "No"she said, "he simply fidgets and hangs upside down". I thought long and hard and decided to tackle my son at home.

When we talked about the problems my son got very very emotional and stated that the lady hated him, he was a good boy he said and tried to talk to the lady but she was not interesting to talk to so he gave up. He said he tried to remember his apron but simply forgot he was very sorry. Our son sobbed for the first time in his young life, what kind of a mother was I ?, I felt horrible. We hugged and I rocked him to sooth him from his sudden sadness. I could not actually get my head around the problem at all. At home we baked, I never bought processed foods and we did art play and he always wore an apron. It did later occur to me that actually , I produced the apron and dressed him in it. Now, this child is still three years old, a baby, yes he looked bigger, but he was actually a young child of three. My husband and I actually giggled a little at our seemingly silly problem and put it behind us.

However not all things will go away and this problem, got worse. Our son, who was so happy, was becoming so sad and withdrawn, but he still walked into school looking back at me daily. He will be all right I told myself, he will grow to love it. This however did not happen and to makes matters worse the teacher really got very annoyed at him, she shouted at him most of the time becoming very frustrated at this child who still forgot the same small rules and who never sat still for a story time. At home during story time, the same could be said. He would hang upside down or lie on the carpet with his teddy bear but I did not think that was unusual.

One day I arrived at the school and the teacher hailed me from the other side of the school yard, all the other mothers looking on. What now, I thought, exasperated at this terrible nursery teacher. She walked toward me and declared in a very loud voice she was having great difficulty coping with her morning sessions with my son, he would not remember his apron and mixed sand and water together , he talked constantly to the others and the last straw for her was when he took the dolls pram up the ramp. I looked at my son who was sobbing, I felt like a crazy mother, what was I to do . I brought a healthy, lovely, intelligent child to this school who never ever cried and what had happened. Now I had a child who sobbed constantly, grew increasingly clingy to me, and why, because of aprons and prams and a teacher I thought had a few problems of her own.

I looked at my son who was wet from the water play and who was sobbing. Not crying you understand, simply sobbing, and this teacher was shouting her disgust and telling my son off again. I asked her not to shout and advised her no one shouted at home, he simply was not used to it. As she continued saying it was difficult to teach the other children I was becoming a little annoyed myself. I held up my hand to signal her to stop, and I told her very quietly he would not be coming to nursery again , not tomorrow or any other day. She looked at me in horror, then she smiled and said she thought it was for the best.

I took my son by the hand and we walked away from the nursery school. I thought this action was for the best as the teacher was obviously finding it hard and was really very frustrated by my son. The next morning we went back to our routine, I felt sad for him knowing he was missing out especially with playing with other children but I can tell you my lovely, very happy son returned. He was simply a joy, intelligent, inquisitive, tiring but in a very good way. He was most of all and importantly to our family the happy child we had previously known. He was however a little wary now of others.

We as parents decided to send our children, obviously the older two first and later this would include our youngest son to a nearby village school. We based this decision on several events but mainly our thinking was that the village school they were at now was very small. In the middle sons class there were six children, he was top of the class they said but you can see that six children, was hardly a cross section of society. The nearby village school had around twenty five children in every class, the children moved up yearly, the head teacher we loved as she was very intelligent and caring. She was also interested in children applying for the local grammar school, if they took an outside examination. Both our other sons benefited from this move of schools and they both passed the examination for the grammar school which is one of the best in the country. We never regretted this decision.

The head teacher of the school saw our youngest son daily as he waited for his older brothers, he was hardly missable. He was tall, at four years old nearly the size of a six year old. He was very blond and chatted to the head teacher constantly about his day, his insects, anything. She was very excited at the prospect of having such a bright child in her school. This knowledge placed all our minds at rest and we were sure our past problems would be just that, that they would remain firmly in the past.

STARTING JUNIOR SCHOOL.

In the year that our youngest son turned five years old he was to start junior school. He was born in early January so at the age of four he started school in early September. At first he went in the mornings later to be followed by full days. He was very excited, he loved the school, he knew some of the teachers through his brothers time there, so he was eager to become a big boy and learn more.

He was to wear a uniform which had to be thought through, firstly because he was so tall and secondly because he found doing buttons and zips etc.. very difficult indeed. So we devised, what we thought, was a foul proof plan. Elastic replaced zips and buttons, rehearsals taught him to change his uniform, in particular his shirt, into PE gear without opening any buttons. With the simple action of pulling it over his head. Socks were no problem as from a very young age he simply refused, point blank, to wear them. In his own words, if it was good enough for Albert Einstein ,then it is good enough for him. I found it difficult to justify any argument to that statement and thought it unimportant anyway. Our only problem was the small black PE pumps that were obligatory, he could not put them on, so, we told a white lie. I advised the school his feet were so wide and big they simply did not make them in his size, and so, I bought non marking trainers with Velcro fastenings. Although I have to admit to change his clothes himself still took a long time, I felt very pleased with our forward planning and I was sure this would enable him to have the greatest success.

On the first day of school, I drove a very excited boy. His view of school was a very positive one as he had been many times and loved learning anything. The first class was the reception class which was simply a little learning and playing scenario very similar to a nursery situation. After the first few weeks the teacher produced some simple work sheets, these are normal for a four year old learning to write. A curvy c for instance, the idea he traced around the c and copied it later.

Now, just to set the record straight, you may, I am sure be asking the simple question, "if he is such a bright child, why has the mother not taught him to write his letters and numbers before school age"? Well the answer to that is, I did try, he knows them all, well to clarify he can count to infinity, and he is at the age of four, super articulate, in fact I have never ever heard a child that is so articulate at four years old. But, and here it comes, I just could not teach him, not at all. He could dictate the most amazing stories with me writing, he can add in his head, but he cannot write anything. I felt sure there was some teachers special knack that I did not know about that would solve the small problem. So, back to these sheets, well first he could not hold the pencil properly, when I tried again and again to show him he would pass the pencil to the other hand. I thought OK maybe he is left handed just like his father. The teacher said not to worry he would find his own way forward soon. However we soon found out that would not be the case. In October, we had a small parent teacher talk when the teacher said not to worry it would all come together, the problem they were finding difficulty with was dressing or undressing changing in fact for PE, water play, Art etc..She said it took him so long that the teachers help, aided him and the lessons were nearly over by the time he was ready. As for our son he became a little frustrated and kept asking if he was a naughty boy, for which I would hurriedly answer of course not love. However I was beginning to worry slightly at this point. I am a mother of three, I was not in the habit of worrying unnecessarily. I believe all children should take as much time as possible to grow, develop and change as a childhood only happens once, but even I was beginning to question now, what could possibly be holding him back from making progress in certain areas.

I had a good friend who was a teacher and I asked if she would help me privately, and maybe teach him the alphabet, some key first words. She also had older children and said I was worrying too much. I looked again at my tall bright boy and decided that I was just like others, just because he looked like a seven year old, I should not expect him to be one, he was only four not yet five. At this, I laughed at myself and dismissed any worry I had.

As he turned five years of age, some restructuring was taking place at the school. The reception teacher was pregnant and the class room was very small, so it was decided that all children who were five would move up and the younger remain thus distributing the group. I had no problem with anything they did, who does at this stage, I did not know the new teacher,but, I was not worried, I had great respect for the school. But during the first week of the new class, when I arrived to collect my son I was asked to talk to the head teacher. Now I admit that for a millisecond I did think, oh please not again. But I was to learn that the teacher had real concerns. She advised me that not to worry, but, the new teacher had noticed that during a routine PE class, my son did not perform well. She was worried but thought there could be ways to help him. I was a little shocked, but as I have said in the past he was a very tall, big boy. He was always clumsy but I thought, that was because he was so tall and his mind elsewhere instead of watching where he was going.

THE DIAGNOSIS (DYSPRAXIA).

The head mistress told me that she had contacted the school doctor and that the school doctor would see him at a local health centre tomorrow. The fact the appointment was for tomorrow should have rung alarm bells, but it didn't. I thought that was good of them seeing my son so quickly.

The next day we arrived at the local health centre to see the school doctor. Guess who the doctor was ?. It was the same lady who saw him for his developmental appointments. She had him do simple things, draw a circle, stand up, sit down, stuff that seemed a little silly to me at the time, However I was shocked to realise that he could not do any of the things she asked of him. She asked me, "how has this child got to this age, and these motor control difficulties not been seen before ?". I said "sorry !". She repeated the statement again her tone a little off, like I was a bad mother, which I immediately resented. I reminded her that it was her who saw him at the developmental stages, she was the qualified doctor not me. She looked at me long and hard and then said quietly, "your son appears to have a problem with his motor control, is he clumsy?" " Yes" I said. "Well, I will send him to see a specialist in the field and then we will get to the route of the problem". "Thank you" I said and dutifully walked out of the room.

When I arrived home I discussed the doctors statements with my husband, we decided that we had a lovely happy child so what was the worst they were going to say. We awaited the appointment with interest but, decided both of us would attend the next one. We did not wait long, we received two future appointments in the post, one for a neurologist and one for a professor in paediatrics. We went to our local big city, first to the neurologist who was a very abrupt lady, she declared that, he should firstly see the paediatrician, she did not see why he had been sent to her, as his problems were not in her field. This information actually made us happy, as you only need a neurologist when something is very wrong. Right!.

When the second appointment came, we were a little worried as the previous lady was very officious and distant, not a very helpful combination when you as a parent are a little confused as to why you are there. We waited in a room, my husband and my son and I until, in came a man. He was a very nice, very warm and friendly person, the complete opposite of the previous doctor. The chairs were along the edge of the modest room, and there was space in the middle. He first shook our hands, and then he introduced himself to our son, who, declared he was pleased to meet him also. The doctor then did the strangest thing, he sat on the floor and asked our son to do the same. He asked him if he would like to play a game of copying, and did he understand how to copy, Our son loved games and gleefully said "yes of course".

The doctor first placed his hands on his head, our son copied. He then placed his hands on his nose, our son copied. The doctor stood upright and asked our son to do the same. The most startling thing happened then, our son shuffled to the nearest chair and used the chair to leaver himself up. The doctor said "very good, now we can sit on the floor again and I want you to stand up like me, use only you legs". Well, he tried to stand but was unable so, he leant forward and stood using his hands and knees. We were shocked as he was definitely, unable, to do this simple task.

The doctor moved quickly on to the next task, ignoring the fact our son could not do the previous one. He asked him to stand on one leg, balance in fact, arms out or down. Our son to our horror failed again. Then the other leg, he continued to fail. We sat quietly watching, wondering what bad parents we must be to allow our son to get to five years old and not notice this problem. Whatever of course this problem was.

The examination continued in the hall way of the hospital. In all hospital hallways there are coloured lines; these lines people follow in order to find the correct route to different places within the hospital. The doctor walked along one line, our son,and us watching. Our son tried to copy, but he was unable to stay on the line at all, in fact, he wobbled so much we thought he would fall down. Then he was asked to walk back along another line. The failure continued, as we continued to look on in shock. He was then asked if he could run, the reply was "yes, but I do not really like to". The doctor asked him if he would run a little for him, simply to the next large doors and back. Well, I can tell you this was distinctly no normal run. (there is that word again, normal). Back inside the room, sitting on the floor, the doctor placed both his hands together as if in prayer. He then kept his palms together and touched in turn each finger to finger, e.g.: baby finger to baby finger and so on. Our son seemed unable to find his opposite finger, another failure.

The doctor took out a piece of paper calmly telling our son he was doing so well, he was very proud of his hard work. He took out a pencil and drew a small circle, he asked my son to copy what he had done. He could not. The doctor drew a large circle and asked him to trace the out line with a different colour, he could not. Our sons line was all over the place. At this stage, our son declared to the doctor he was extremely tired now, he felt he had done enough. He asked if the doctor could finish as he wanted to sit on his fathers knee. The Doctor acknowledged his tiredness, and gave his permission to sit on my husbands lap. Our son climbed up eagerly, snuggled into his father and within minutes was actually asleep.

The Doctor calmly sat on his chair and turned to us. He looked at us for what seemed like ages before he spoke very softly. "Were you aware he had such problems?". I told the Doctor we were aware he was very clumsy, we put that down to the fact he was so tall. I was also aware he could not use a fork and spoon, or knife and fork, but as he was so young, I was not unduly concerned, but now obviously I should have been.

My husband asked the Doctor what he thought the actual problem was. The doctor said that our son had problems with his fine and gross motor skills. He went on to say that in some children these skills are learned almost by copying others, some people use the term parrot fashion, but in other children they find some how there is almost a missing connection or link which prevents a child from learning the skill in this manor. The skill, or fine or gross motor function must be taught in a different way in order for the child to develop.

Most children only show a problem in one of the motor functions. It was he said quite unusual to find a child who had problems with both of his motor functions. Our obvious question next was, "what can we do ?" "First we will request a neurological scan to determine there are no problems we cannot see, then we will request a skilled child physiotherapist to look at him and see if they could work with him to help him progress". We were happy that we could at least do something. He then said something that he may have lived to regret, he said that he would now be our sons Doctor, and if we had other problems or concerns in the future we should ring his secretary. He would then try to see us as soon as possible. We thanked him sincerely for his help and left the hospital.

The appointment for the scan came very quickly and two days later we met a physiotherapist who was wonderful, she worked with children. She told us that she would come into the school to be with our son, she would do motor tests on him and then talk to us again. Our son liked and trusted her, I was very pleased as the appointment with the Doctor had shown us how tired he became during these activities. As he liked her so much I was sure he would try so hard to do well for her.

Next we received another appointment at the School, this appointment was not for our son but for us his parents to discuss the findings. Present at the appointment was the school Doctor, the Paediatrician, The Physiotherapist, the head teacher, the class teacher and us. We were told the neurological scan was good, there were no problems they could see e.g. epilepsy for instance. We were then advised of the physiotherapist fine and gross motor results. We were told our son had scored nil in his fine motor tests and nil in his gross motor tests, the worst they had seen in a long time. We were told our son had a condition called Dyspraxia.

We had never heard the term dyspraxia before and asked what it was. "Basically", they replied, " it is a non development of fine or gross motor skills, it is unusual to get both skills lacking but it can happen in some cases." "The reason for this happening is not always clear, some experts think that it happened during the birth of the child, others believe it to be an hereditary condition."

The class teacher reported that she was unable to get our son to sit on his chair in the normal way, he would slouch, lean hang on the desk, no matter what she said to him he could not sit still it seemed.

It was determined that the next step forward was for the child physiotherapist to work with our son in school every morning for the term of six weeks, to see if improvements can be made, we were assured that this procedure had been very successful in the past with other children and in turn the children had been able to take these new learned skills into the classroom and further into there daily lives thus helping them progress more normally.

We were very grateful for all their help and made our sincere thanks to all parties involved. We left the school with a million questions in our minds, but with the knowledge that all the professionals were helping us and helping our son.

THE FORWARD PLAN.

When we arrived home from the meeting at school our minds were buzzing; Dyspraxia, we had never ever heard of it, neither of us. We decided though that the first thing we should do was to find out more about it. We had a computer all the boys used and today, the first thing we would do is go straight on the internet, but this was fifteen years ago and the internet had a simple explanation, similar to the one we had already been given.

We had the idea to look in the yellow pages, and, in the back of the book there is a list of all organisations, some for single parents, Samaritans, AA and low and behold there was a Dyspraxia organisation. So we made a note of the number and address and soon after tea when the boys were busy doing homework and playing we placed a call to the number. No one answered but we were asked to leave a message, so we did.

Later that evening a gentleman rang us back, we told him of the days events, at first he was quiet and listened intently. He told us a little more than we had bargained for. What he said was another shock, but today sixteen years later, we would like to meet this man and shake his hand. His words to us we felt were emotional and worrying, but we were later to find they were in fact truthful and only the tip of the iceberg. His words to us drove me as a mother and us as parents to help our son unequivocally. No matter what it took.

The man advised us of a list of books that were available at library's or book stores. He then told us, in our area, there was no Dyspraxia association meeting, but that he could send us information about Dyspraxia. He told us of his daughter who was sixteen and said that in the last two days she had been taken into care, that we should waste no time at all getting school help, as time with these children was of the essence, he stated most of the young adults with Dyspraxia are in full time care of one kind or another. The prisons he said were full of Dyspraxic and Dyslexic youths and adults. This was grave and shocking news for us and a little more than we could take in as our son was simply five years of age and just starting out in life. As his parents we had very high hopes for him, as all parents do for there children. All these years later we realise that the chap must have had an exceptional emotional time with his daughter and that our telephone call coincided with a grave time for his family.

After the call, sitting shocked I made plans to be up to date with all the information I could about Dyspraxia. There was no way we would loose our son into care. We had talked to the man for a long time and shared his sadness and pain. With each word of comfort to him it only reaffirmed our solidarity to provide for our son, whatever it took.

The next day the physiotherapist came to school, she worked with our son for six weeks, over and over again, daily repeating exercises. She gave us a plan for home life, this involved weekends walking on the beaches with Wellington's on. Pushing prams , wheelbarrows, shopping trolly's in the stores. This all seems silly stuff right. Well you would be wrong. These simple exercises would send our son into shreds of tears as he found them all so difficult. But we persevered, we even bought a special wheelbarrow for his tractor and we wasted no opportunity at all.

The six weeks came and went and they reported some improvements, we could not see any, actually, but they were the experts. At the end of the six weeks, as some progress had been made I asked for it to continue, they said funding for children was only six weeks long. I said I would pay, but they said it was impossible. They could be reported to the health associations and they would get into trouble. I tried private organisations but I was told the same tale.

This was my first real stumbling block with the professionals, if progress is being made, well my un-professional insides tell me to continue with what works. Well the answer is no, they do not do that. I thought this to be insane myself.

We also made the decision to pay my friend privately to teach our son the letters of the alphabet only, to write if possible the letters and numbers. The teacher also thought it a good idea to teach him to touch type on a computer as she thought this may be his way forward in the future. We thank god for her, she was a blessing. She worked with our son, saying toe by toe, no rush. It may take three years to learn the alphabet of 26 letters. We did not care and we are thankful for her expert insight and her softly softly approach to learning.

How was school finding things you may ask?. Well the answer was they were finding it very difficult indeed. The teachers help from the reception class was drafted into the next classroom in a vain bid to help the teacher, but to no avail. The class was thirty pupils full, all learning differently. Two and a half class years of ability all with their own problems, and our son. Our son who could not sit still, could not write, read, draw, do maths or change for PE unaided. Even lunch times were a problem as our son did not eat properly, but chose to use his fingers. In fact he failed all day long, from the beginning to end. This lovely happy little boy was no more, he cried all the time. Every evening when he came home he would beg me not to send him to fail again the next day. In his class children were seven, six and five years old. Now anyone knows that there is a vast difference between a seven year olds ability and a six and five year olds. My son was so bright, he looked toward these children who could do most things and just felt worse, it made him feel more of a failure. The other children ostracised him, as they knew he was different . This did nothing to help his plight.

Around the eighth week since the meeting at school the head teacher told me they were desperate and although they had rules and protocol to follow with the education board with regard to help for children like my son, this situation was urgent so she had called an emergency meeting for the following week to discuss any way forward.

OBTAINING THE STATEMENT OF EDUCATION FROM THE LOCAL EDUCATION AUTHORITY.

After a brief meeting with the head teacher in which the she stated that it would be impossible for the school to continue helping our son unless they received some extra financial help toward teaching him, special books, templates, pencils were needed in order to help him learn at all. It was not just financial help the school required but guidance from a specialist as this was the only child they had ever had with Dyspraxia in their school. In the past the education authority would send these children to a special needs school who were experts in dealing with these specific learning difficulties. Now in this modern day approach to teaching, they prefer to integrate the child within a normal (that word again) school. She advised me that all schools, actually, already receive a budget for special needs children, but! what this means in essence is that it may go toward providing ramps at entrances, or that some children have a small problem reading, writing or with maths. They require extra time with someone who can read to them more, or, who can explain things in a different way, until they get the idea. This however was not the case with our son, she explained, that he would never get the idea, unless he had access to a special needs qualified teacher who was used to dyspraxic children, and could advise the school on different teaching methods and approaches . The school budget did not cover such expenses, this specialist teacher would have to come from from the special needs education authority. She stressed the despair of the, school, of the class teacher, and of my son. I told her that I would get them the help somehow, I just did not know how at this time. The emergency meeting was set for the end of the week so it was necessary for me to become educated in these matters quickly.

This is what I did and how I did it. I hope this information helps someone in some way in the future.

To become educated in the matters of special needs education, I took time off work and spoke to everyone I could. I considerd the experts, to be the parents of children who face difficulties at any school, and, who need to deal with the education authority in order to get help for their child in any school. I listed the people I knew who had children with any kind of special need. I then made appointments one after the other and asked them of the process, the time things take, how approachable these people were, and if they had any advise they could give me. I was given a small leaflet by the school which advised a route for parents with concerns, but, if the leaflet was to be believed, it could take around two years at least for the process to be completed. This time span was unacceptable to me and the school, everyone needed immediate help in the form of money and advise.

The story from other parents is I am afraid a very grim one. They all talk of tears, arguments, unapproachable local authority special needs education staff, difficult educational psychologists. The list seemed to be endless.

Now in my job I was aware that all solicitors specialise in different areas, a little like doctors. Some specialise in land and housing laws, some in divorce, some in medical compensation. I am sure you understand the concept. Some solicitors actually specialise in education law and some in special needs education law. Time was short so I found a solicitor in the greater London area, at this time we lived in Lancashire. So I paid for a telephone interview, the price was just less than £100 . This is what she told me.

The local authority special needs Education authority may state they do not like to label a child, if a child gets labelled, i.e. given a diagnosis, this can act almost like a stigma and follow the child for years, even holding the child back in the future.

You need an actual diagnosis, written on the statement of education so that the child will receive the correct help toward his or her specific learning disorder, for now and in the future. If you do not have a diagnosis, push for one. Have that diagnosis written on the statement in black and white. Then the child will receive help toward his or her education specifically targeting his or her needs. This statement follows the child through school and is amended yearly.

The Special needs education authority may say that they can only give minimum hours to help, as there are other children and they are working within budgeting constraints. All schools have to work within a budget, and without exception so does the local education authority however, this is their problem not yours.

Every child has a right to be taught to reach his or her full potential, keep repeating this statement within the meeting. Ensure this is enclosed on the statement somewhere.

Did you know that the actual average reading age in England is only eight years old, this is true. If your child reaches this age in their ability to read, and is eight years of age and over, they may deem it sufficient and withdraw some of the help in some way. THIS IS WRONG.

You do not care about the population of England only your child, and if further help means reaching a fuller potential, then more help should be given.

Also, she advised me that the education authority may be overruled by a medical opinion if the authority's withdrawal of support ,in some way, could be detrimental to the child, so ask the medical experts to every meeting. If they are unable to attend, obtain a letter or statement off them regarding the child's condition.

A child's emotional condition is important also, at school and at home. The education of a child is not just catering to English and maths. It is about the whole child, his or her emotional condition is just as important.

Ensure the teachers are at the meetings. The head teacher, class teacher, anyone who may come into contact with your child and can give an account of your child's needs. You have a right to invite these people.

You have a right to legal council also, if you require it, even your MP can help you. Find out who your local MP is and draft a letter or visit them in their free surgery's. They will be only to happy to help you if they can.

If you are emotional from the stress of the situation and you think there is a possibility you will cry at the meeting my advise would be to contact the Parent partners association. They will send a parent with you, who can speak for you, and the child without emotion. (I admit that I am a controlling person and as such I was unable to use the parent partners association, believing that no one could speak for my child as I could) However it is better to be labelled a pushy parent rather than an over emotional one. The education authority may cease to listen to you if you become over emotional in there presence.

You have the right for the child to be present , I do not think this is a good idea personally as usually the child feels bad enough without everyone discussing them. Only you can decide according to your situation the best route to take.

Lastly her advise was that although the authority have a time table of events and situations which they like to follow prior to giving any help, be advised that they also have to deal urgently in an emergency situation. If you can show there is such an emergency then they have to give help the next day if need be.

A piece of knowledge imparted to me via a mother who had a son of nineteen years old, who had special needs from the age of four was;... do not allow your child to be a paper exercise. Take a photograph with you and place it outwards on the meeting table. Any statement you hand in attach a photograph of the child on the top of every copy. This will remind the officials involved that this is a child they refer to, not simply a paper exercise.

(I wish any parent good luck and our best wishes).

So with the meeting set for the end of the week, all the people invited that needed to be, all statements taken and photographs made we decided exactly what we wished to say to the authority on behalf of our son and the school. We drafted a rough copy of notes to keep me on track when I spoke to them, just in case the meeting went in another direction. This was useful to us. Another thing we did was to write down a list of questions we required answering.

The meeting began,and everyone introduced themselves to everyone else. I had a feeling most of them knew each other anyway, but the pleasantries began. The paediatrician accepted my invitation and brought a document from the physiotherapy unit for us which was passed around. The teachers were asked of any problems they had and the head teacher said the situation was extremely urgent and advised the meeting of their problems and worries. Then it was our turn to be asked. We advised the Education authority that all the teachers were struggling but most of all, so was our son, at this stage at the age of five and a half he could not read or write anything. He struggled to hold a pencil, to sit still on the chair . He struggled with the simplest of instructions, we thought this was due to the stress he was under. We advised everyone at the meeting that he was now very aware of his complete failure in all tasks, and as such we felt he was an emotional time bomb. He was internalising his stressful situation and as such he had developed a tremor in his hands, this was visible for all to see making writing or any fine motor task impossible. We advised them he cried at home all the time and that this was since he had come to school; prior to school he was a happy child. His walk was visibly different also, he walked on the balls of his feet, to an onlooker it appeared he was walking on his tip toes. The doctor confirmed his diagnosis and went on to state the severity of the dyspraxia. The solicitor was correct , the authority did take special notice of the doctors words. They said they would take all this under advisement and someone higher would recommend a level of hours needed for the statement if any. I asked them how and why my son was so bright and how he knew so much information, about so many things if he could not read. This question remained unanswered.

The meeting broke up and we were advised that they would provide us with a statement of available hours within days. They kept their word and the following week on the Tuesday the authority representative

SQUARE PEG ROUND HOLE

called to the school and offered us Ten hours extra help, plus two and a half hours with a higher level teacher. This made a total of twelve and a half hours to begin immediately. The paperwork to be finalised at a later date. The higher level teacher would come to school every week and work with our son one on one for two and a half hours, the other ten hours would be with a teachers assistant, who would be employed especially for our son, who would sit with him and help him in ways that would be set out in the educational statement.

I knew from talking to other families this hourly rate was very high. We were elated that all the hard work had seemed to pay off.

THE HELP ARRIVES.

Over the next couple of weeks quite large changes took place at school.

We were introduced to a lady in her early twenties who was applying for the position of teaching assistant. This person would, if we liked her, work along side of our son for ten hours weekly. The young lady seemed very nice indeed and we had no objections to her helping our son, we were in fact quite shocked, but pleased ,that we were consulted on this matter. The lady did work in another class higher in the school for a few hours a week and as the school knew her well and trusted her they had thought her ideal for the position.

We liked her because she was a very calm person, quiet and caring. We were sure our son would respond well to her. Over the next couple of years the two of them formed a good trusting relationship.

We were also introduced to the higher level teacher who seemed nice, she had brought with her an ' individual education plan', this document formed the way forward, for the school teacher and the assistant. It stated separately each individual learning idea for our son. The higher special needs teacher would then come to school, work one on one with him in an attempt to teach him letters, reading, writing etc...

The document stated small objectives, the idea behind this is that if he could succeed at a small thing, then his self esteem would grow and everyone could build on this. Similar to that of a wall, good foundations mean a good strong wall for the future. To us as parents the idea sounded very good. Two of these small objectives written in the plan haunted our son for years to come, the ideas sounded good at the time, but, time proved they were never possible. These two statements were as follows;...

1. To remain seated in the class chair, at the desk, with both feet on the floor for one minute.

2. To learn to eat with a knife and fork.

The class teacher did feel a little better because all of her time did not have to be directed toward our son, she was now able to try to teach the rest of the class and she felt that at last he was getting some individual input.

The following week we saw the paediatrician again, we updated him on the progress at the school. He was very happy that something was happening to help the situation. He asked our son about the assistant, did he like her?, and how were things?. Our shock was what our son said next, he stated he liked the new lady lots who sat with him at his desk, but, he hated the new teacher who kept showing him letters and numbers he could not remember. He went on to say the class teacher and the other pupils at the school hated him and he did not understand why he had to keep going to the school. He cried and begged the doctor to tell us not to send him again. He said he had stopped eating at school in the lunch times and that he would never eat there again. He told us all he had planned his way home and the next time he was unhappy , he would run away from school.

We all sat quite quiet for a moment absorbing this information. The the doctor asked our son to colour a picture for him, he handed him a printed picture and some crayons. Whilst our son coloured the doctor told us he knew of another doctor, a clinical psychologist, whom he trusted, and who worked with children like our son. He said he felt it was imperative that our son talk to her as soon as would be possible. He would talk to her about us and our son and request that she saw him on a regular basis. We agreed and thanked him for all his help, he stated he would see us in three weeks time to check again that all was well.

When we arrived home our son went to his room and we sat looking at each other, a little in shock yet again. I wanted as much help for my son as possible, but I have to say I was very nervous. I had never in my life had any dealings with any psychologists, and, I did not know what to expect. I had nothing to hide, none of my family did, but questions still flew around in my head. Would they think all this was my fault?. How deep would this person pry into our lives?. For some reason I felt this step would be far to intrusive for me to handle.

I can tell you that sixteen years on this lady was invaluable to us as parents and most importantly to our son. He grew to trust her above all the people he saw over the years. If you are given the opportunity for your child to see a child psychologist, do not hesitate. The good this lady did for our family is unmeasurable. They can listen to your child in confidence, we all need this at desperate times in our lives, and for some, those times come sooner than others. They can advise you on strategies of coping with a child's despair. She gave us simple ways to help build up his self esteem. We will never be able to thank her enough for everything. The waiting lists for child psychologists in England are very long indeed, so my advice is if you get offered one try to keep them for as long as possible.

The appointment to see the child psychologist came within the next two days, I took my son out of school and we drove to see her. She saw the two of us first and then my son alone. After she had seen my son she invited me back into the room, she told me that she would see my son weekly for a while as she felt he was in crisis. She went on to explain that children like him saw only a black and white situation. There were no grey areas for these children, he would love it or hate it nothing in between. Our aim for the immediate future was to try to change his statements. So, if he said, "they all hate me". I should say, "maybe they are all a little unhappy today, they do not hate you, they are just unhappy today". This changing of statements had to be consistent, in order to point out there were always grey areas.

Our son liked the new doctor, he talked about her on the way home saying that she had explained to him about confidentiality, she and he had placed a small cross (signifying a signature), on a confidentiality agreement. This meant he could say anything he wanted and it would never be repeated. She had talked to him as a person and not as a five year old soon to be six. She had praised him for his articulation, his ability at such a young age to express himself fluently, and she thought he was very clever and interesting. He said she was the first adult since starting school that had not treated him like he was stupid, she had agreed with him that his IQ was far superior to most children around his age. He had told her that at times, because he could not read, the school placed him in a group of children who had difficulty reading and doing mathematics. He added that the group of five children were made up of children who were not very clever. He could not understand why he had to work with this group of children, they were not very bright and had nothing important to say on any subject.

We continued to see this doctor who worked tirelessly with our son.

The Dyspraxia association had contacted me to advise me that a very famous professor who was doing studies into dyspraxia was coming to the north of England to give a talk at a university . I approached the class teacher and invited her to come with me to the university to hear the gentleman speak on the subject. I thought this would give me, and more importantly her, a greater insight into dyspraxia. My hope was that she would become a little less frustrated with my son in the future, having gained a greater understanding of the problems he was facing. The teacher agreed to accompany me to the university. It was a very interesting evening for both of us. I learned that dyspraxia is a new term for this motor control problem, that years ago in fact, was called 'minimal brain dysfunction'. The doctors and all those associated with the disorder thought the older term to be derogatory and the newer term to be a lot nicer. Another eye opener for me was that the professor stated that dyspraxia usually went hand in hand with other things like dyslexia. The definition for dyslexia is impaired ability to read, not caused by low intelligence. Non-technical name is word blindness.

THE STRUGGLE AT SCHOOL CONTINUES.

School continues to be a complete struggle from the age of six years to the age of seven and a half years, the whole system seemed to be against us. Due to the new information regarding dyslexia being linked to dyspraxia, we requested they test our son to ascertain if he had dyslexia, as there was such a difference between his articulation, knowledge and his ability to read and write. The tests for dyslexia took less than two hours. Of course, the test came back to reveal that he was very dyslexic indeed.

I felt very angry that the so called professional special needs teachers, who knew all about dyspraxia, had not thought to test our son previously. In my view the delay in testing him for dyslexia had prevented him from being able to be taught correctly, and get the help he needed. Many things have changed with regard to teaching dyslexic children. Special coloured sheets can be placed on the books to prevent the words from literally running around the pages. Phonic teaching is available, and lastly, it is possible to have a special eye test. During this test, the specialist optician can discover how the child responds to different colours. All children are very different and sometimes a combination of colours work better.

We took our son to such an optician and he had lovely glasses made for him, he felt so much calmer in these glasses, he choose to wear them daily. (a combination of thirty two colours made up the lenses)

During the next meeting at school his statement was increased in hours to 17 and all the staff at school were still saying they were unable to cope.

This next paragraph is written from my sons perspective of school at the age of 7years old.

"Every night I have nightmares because I hate school so much, I always have the same dream. I am running to a large tree in the middle of a field. On this tree are numbers and letters and I try to jump up for them but I cannot reach them. I see the faces of the teachers looking at me, shouting at me, screaming at me and I wake up screaming.

In the mornings,I try to dress myself but all my clothes just get twisted up and I am so sad and tired. My mummy makes me breakfast but I feel to sick to eat it, when I try to eat I have to run to the sink to be sick. The sick is just acid and phlegm in my throat. I cry and cry but I know mummy will make me go anyway. I think about the noise of school, other people and the smells and I have to run to be sick again. I climb in the car next to mummy and I know she loves me as she talks calmly to me, but it does not help me. I feel very alone.No one understands what it feels like to fail at everything I do. I watch the other children doing maths, english, reading, history, science, PE and I cannot do anything, nothing. I cannot write my name, I cannot read at all I am stupid, I feel trapped. I shake all the time, the more worried I am the more I shake. The other children know I am different and they hate me, they pick on me because I am thick. I watch the teachers talk about me and I hate them all, I would run away, but I have no where to run to. I sit in the car going to school and I am sick again in the footwell. Mummy does not say anything because she knows this happens every day. I ask god every day to help me but he does not help, I wish I could die".

From the age of 6 to the age of 7years, school was very difficult for all involved and more so for our son. At the age of 21years, our son still finds it very difficult to discuss this period in his life. To him it was a very bleak time indeed, he discusses at times the possibility that he may train to be a teacher, in the vain hope that he can spare a child the trauma the journey, he feels, he did not survive, but that has scarred him for life.

As life daily becomes this traumatic routine of sadness and failure, we are given a small miracle. This miracle came in the form of a doctor who was specialising in special needs. The clinical psychologist knew the doctor and discussed with him the possibility of looking at our son and talking to us. We went to the hospital, with our son for a meeting. The doctor advised us of his research and talked at great length to our son with us present.

He then looked directly at our son and asked him if he would do some tests for him and possibly aid him in his research. Our son agreed readily, the tests would mean him being at the hospital daily for as long as it took. This would mean he would not be able to go to school until the tests were completed. They were going to first of all test his IQ, then they were going to look into how he learnt, specifically how he digested information. Was this visually, audibly ?.

The results of the tests were absolutely mind-blowing. They showed our sons IQ to be high, very high, possibly higher than the teachers who were trying to teach him. The tests proved that the knowledge he had gained had been via visual and audible skills. His visual skills not quite that of a photographic memory , but almost. We were given a report, which detailed that during the IQ tests, our son had become bored and he had actually started to test the doctors. At this time, due to our sons young age, those tests were abandoned.

Armed with this report and another report from the clinical psychologist, in which she stated clearly that our son was becoming 'School Phobic' ,we requested an emergency meeting. At this meeting, we were able to prove 'absolutely' that our sons IQ and his actual ability was cavernous. At the age of seven and a half years he was completely word and number blind. No progress had been made since the first emergency meeting at the age of five years old. We stated that the education authority had a duty of care toward our son in order to help him reach his full potential. They also have a duty of care to look to the 'whole child', not just the education of that child. We demanded full time hours stating that the school needed help in these exceptional circumstances. We also requested some of these hours to be of a higher level teacher who specialised in dyslexic children.

We were given full time hours with no dispute at all. The school took on another full time nursery assistant teacher who was employed full time to sit next to our son. Her job was to scribe for him, during all his lessons. He was not asked to write during any lesson, this pressure was now lifted. He was also provided with a computer which he used in the class to allow him to try to complete some tasks alone.

For the first time in his life our son produced stories which were amazing. He told the story and the assistant wrote his words. At the age of eight our son had a poem published, an amazing feat for any child, but especially for one who was unable to write anything.

School life was not completely without trauma, and our son still had nightmares about it. He was still sick every morning and he grew impatient at the assistant who wanted him to phrase things differently, or to write a happier story. He disagreed on points of historical facts and found his peers to be annoying and young. But for the most part, it was a little easier than it had been. These hours stayed with our son until he left junior school and were transferred over to secondary school.

Two years prior to him leaving junior school we were advised to begin looking for a secondary school. We were told we could have any school of our choice, but this proved to be a more difficult task than we expected.

Armed with his personnel education plan and his 30 hour statement we started to visit all the very large schools. The truth is that non of these schools have a right to refuse you but when the head of the special needs department in these schools say, "we are sorry but we could not accommodate your child" you do begin to despair a little again. However we are and always will be very grateful to them for there complete honesty.

We eventually chose a smaller church of England school, chosen because they had a separate special needs department and the school was a very family orientated school. We liked their ethos and as religion and moral values were important to our son we thought it was the most likely to be successful.

HOME LIFE TO THE AGE OF 11 YEARS OLD.

Home life for our son and for all of us had to be very different from school life. Everyone needs to be able to come home and feel that home is their sanctuary from the harshness of the world.

After our son started school and he began to get older, and more aware of his failings academically, he started to change. This once bundle of personality and laughter became a mixed up and emotional wreck. We followed the guidance of the professionals for quite a while but home life was becoming very depressing for the entire family, so as parents of three children we decided that changes had to be made. For better or for worse these are the changes we made.

At the age of five and a half years, when things first started to get very difficult at school, we observed our son and realised that he had no friends. Our other boys were at the grammar school and very busy with their lives, they were of a similar age and although they tried hard with their younger brother, just like the teachers at school they could not completely understand his problems and his complete internalisation of his situation. They both loved him dearly but a younger brother who cried continually became tiresome. We decided to purchase a dog, not just any dog but a special one that our son helped to choose. That was large, placid and could be a good friend in the country side setting we lived in. After visiting several dog shows as a family, we settled on the breed of Italian Spinoni. We found a breeder in Lancaster, visited them and even though they had no puppies at this time we pre ordered one.

Several months later we received a phone call stating that the mother was pregnant, we called to see them with a video camera and our son filmed the mother whilst we were made to feel welcome as a family ,and enjoyed a day in the sun. A few months later we received a phone call saying the puppies were born. We drove to see them and our son chose one. It was a male dog, and he decided to call him Dino, after Dino Ferrari. He was completely white and stunning. He had to remain with his mother for a while but our son had something lovely to look forward to . A few weeks later we brought Dino home. He grew and grew and was in the end around ten stones in weight. he was pure white with an amber nose and eyes. They became inseparable, he was a loving pet to the entire family, but, a friend and confidant to our youngest son. Dino was always waiting for him to come home. Dino lived to be thirteen years old and we all miss him today.

My husband had the wonderful idea of creating a bedroom on a low level especially for our son. This bedroom was in the attic of our house and ran the whole length of the building. He created lots of storage under the eves using plastic boxes with wheels on them. In each box we placed different items, and on each box we drew pictures of the items in the box. For example for trousers we drew a pair of trousers, (I am sure you get the idea). We bought our son a large TV which sat very low to the floor. Our son had great difficulty sleeping at nights due to frequent nightmares, and on one of these occasions he discovered that during the night the BBC ran the Open University courses. We allowed him to watch this every night, if he wished, so long as he was quiet and did not disturb the other members of the household. This worked well for all the members of the family.

Our son had a problem eating with a knife and fork. It soon became obvious he was never going to achieve this fine motor skill. In a bid to solve a problem and prevent sadness at home the whole household decided to eat with a fork only. We did not see any problem in doing so.

Our son also struggled with his food. He became obsessed with eating correctly, the correct diet, minerals and vitamins etc....He became very focused on the contents of the food we eat, how animals are reared and the antibiotics and growth hormones they are given. At the tender age of five years, we allowed our son to become a vegetarian. He did not eat meat of any kind, he did not eat dairy products, swapping dairy for soya and meat for tofu and quorn. The agreement was that as long as we gave him a full balanced diet of vegetables, salad, pulses,nuts etc.....and that he never refused anything, he could remain a vegetarian as long as he wanted. One set of grandparents worried about his growth, but I can report that at the age of 21years he is 6feet 7inches tall. He is very slim and very healthy. The remainder of the household did eat meat at this time, but now we are all vegetarians and I can report that he was correct, it is the healthiest way to eat as long as the diet is varied. The lunch time problem at school was solved instantly because he could now take a packed lunch full of fruit and finger foods. No need for a knife and fork any more.

We encouraged our son just to learn to enjoy home life whenever possible. On the weekends when we were not going on holiday we allowed him just simply to be. He enjoyed his room, his things and his own time. We never asked him to get dressed, do errands, do chores. He could be found in his pyjamas at lunchtime and again at bedtime. This allowed him to have no stressful dressing. He only dressed if he wished to leave the house.

Our son had a great problem with trust. He only trusted his immediate family. It was not possible to employ any kind of child minder and both I and his father worked full time. His father made the incredible sacrifice of working permanent nights. This allowed me, his mother to take him to school and his father to collect him, in this way he was always with one of us and not a stranger.

We tried to encourage him to do different things. This was difficult as he was very fond of his own personal boundaries. He was happier on the computer, in his room than anywhere else. We took him horse riding as we had been told for some children with sensory problems this was a good activity. He loved this hobby and all the animals at the farm.

We purchased several different instruments, guitars, several drums. All of which he has today, but, he bought a didgeridoo, a deep toned native Australian wind instrument. During a holiday in France he taught himself to play this instrument, he is very good at it.

My husband went to a Canoeing school and got his teachers licence. From being quite young he took all three of our children with a friend of his and some other special need youngsters, on the local canals canoeing. For our sons fifteenth birthday he requested a one man canoe and now we are the proud owners of two canoes. Our son is fantastic at this activity.

We did many activities next to and on the water. Our other boys had learnt to swim at a privately run swimming school nearby. They had done very well, they had passed all their badges right up to and including their gold award. As swimming supports the weight, we decided to send our son there to. This was a disaster. We persevered for five months but he simply cried loudly and the swim instructor became very exasperated with him. On one evening session my husband could not stand his despair any longer and he strode into the pool area, retrieved our son and he never went back.

Our son had and has a passion for collecting things, and to be more precise he keeps anything and everything he has ever owned so, collections simply grow from nowhere. As such he has amassed vast collections of all manor of things as his interests have changed over the years. In his younger days his collections were as follows; Hats, coins, stamps, fossils, animal skulls, insects, electrical devises, army memorabilia, specialist teddy bears, original lithographs, tape books, marvel comic original pictures and live animals.

The animals he had were; his dog Dino, a chinchilla, stick insects, a rescued daegu, a guinea pig, a rescued rabbit, two rats and he was insistent that all these animals had the run of the house . To be in essence ,free and shared with two other small dogs belonging the family. So my husband, laid tiles throughout the house, and each door had a cat flap. Each animal went in and out via the cat flaps in each door. He taught the rabbit and guinea pig to use a cat litter tray. He cared lovingly for these animals and always looked after them. I can state they all lived happily together, with the slight exception of the rabbit who continually tried to eat and fell the Christmas tree each year, causing one or two tense moments.

Our other two boys had mountain bikes, as I am sure most boys do. We bought a small first bike for our youngest and the whole family ran alongside of the bike week after week, month after month, year after year. Eventually, he rode the bike, with training wheels, for the first time alone, to the delight of the entire village row at the age of nine years old. This was a fantastic day for him. He continually fell off and the training wheels stayed on the bike for two years more.

Our son had no friends at all, he was never invited to parties at other children's houses. We gave out many invitations but they were never accepted. To help him foster friendships became an obsession of mine. I tried to enrol him in the local beaver/scouts group. Our other sons had been a part of these groups, finally going on to be venture scouts in there late teens. However the local scout leader told me he did not want our son there unless I stayed with him. I was shocked the whole idea was that he could do something, anything without us being there. Our youngest son is a Christian and a proud one. In the nearby town there was a Methodist church which had a boys brigade attached to it. We were not in fact Methodist but one evening my son and I drove to the town, and we observed the group in action. The activities are those similar to a scout group but with a little more marching, and charity in mind etc... The boys brigade call themselves gods army. I asked my son if he would like to join this troupe and he was delighted. The leader was only to happy to have our son become a member. Every Wednesday evening and every Sunday morning I took my son and he loved it. This was the first time he had done activities with other children without us. He had to do work toward badges, learn to march, and learn to play socially. It was very good for him. He had to wear a uniform, trousers, shirt, jumper, hat, tie and polished black shoes. This was the first time he had tried very very hard to maintain a uniform as credits were given for smartness. This was a great success.

The local church had a great problem with their roof and the building was declared unsafe. This meant that all the local church of England services took place in a local hall or in the local old folks home. The normal old man who served at the alter was very ill, so , our son offered to serve for the vicar. He served every service for two years at the local old folks home and at the hall and also another nearby smaller village church on Sunday afternoons. During this time he met another shy boy who, lived locally and had not many friends. They were not close friends, but did occasionally spend time together. A very shy young man could be seen once a year walking through the village, very proudly carrying the cross at the head of the procession.

Finally just a quick word about the holidays we took as a family. Firstly I have to say we had some fantastic holidays. Our youngest son always took a long time to calm down after school had finished, and about three days before the holiday was coming to an end he would begin to get very emotional. We never ever stayed in a hotel or in any similar type of situation. We purchased tents at first, and we went to Wales by the sea for small holidays or to France for longer holidays. On these holidays we did nothing. Well I realise that sounds a very strange thing to say, but we did nothing. A small amount of bike riding, playing in the sea and on the sand but mostly just being together as a family with no pressure to act or be a certain way. In our sons younger life this was a memorable time for him. If you were to talk to him today at 21 years old he would tell you that camping, playing with simple plastic army men, being with his brothers and dog Dino were the happiest times he had as a youngster. He also liked, and likes today the ethos that French or more precisely Mediterranean people have toward children and young people. He loved, and loves today their spontaneous outbursts, if they are sad, angry or happy. He thinks British people are far two reserved and grumpy toward the young. Perhaps as a nation we have a little to learn from our Mediterranean neighbours?.

PART 2

THE FIRST DAYS OF SECONDARY SCHOOL.

School was a subject none of our family ever mentioned during school holidays. We preferred to believe that if we did not mention the subject, our youngest would forget to worry about it. This of course is a ludicrous notion. Especially when he was shortly to move on to secondary school. If it was mentioned, we said things like, "Its going to be really great, new children, new teachers, fantastic, a brand new beginning".

He was worried though, obviously, the school was about thirty times larger than his previous junior school. He never reacted well to any change,and this was going to be a major one. He was to wear a full uniform, trousers, tie, jacket the works. He was very proud of this fact as he loved to look smart. We had purchased an apple mac ibook, a titanium one. This was a new computer which we thought he would be able to carry easily to the different classrooms. The special needs department was in a separate building from the main school, the two buildings were connected via a courtyard. Whilst most of the lessons were to take place in the special needs department ,some of the others would be within the main building.

On the second day of school, the special needs teacher asked to see us, she stated that the junior school had sent on paperwork about our son, and, in this paperwork were the results of our sons government SATS test.

These tests were designed by the government to tell the schools and parents exactly what each child had achieved, as they reached new levels throughout their school lives. I can vaguely remember our sons entire junior school preparing for SATS week, I never bothered myself about these tests, as far as we were concerned, we had far greater worries at the time. The government states that each child should be able to do well in these tests, as marks are given for writing your name, the date, handwriting, spelling, correct answers etc..Each SATS test is based on the subject matter the child should have been taught that year.

The teacher advised us that our son had in fact scored 'nil' in his SATS tests. We were not in fact shocked at this information, our son was word and number blind!, This means he could not read anything, and he could not write anything at the age of eleven. This had previously been explained to the school, hence his statement containing thirty hours. The teacher explained that he was the first child, to score nil, in Lancashire area, in the SATS tests. Again,we were not shocked, but she was. She then continued by saying that he would have to have extra lessons in order to bring him on a little quicker.

I immediately expressed my concerns at this attitude of hers, with any normal (that word again) child, yes, this would normally be the correct approach. But for a child who was school phobic, dyspraxic, dyslexic and did not react well to any change, I did not agree that this was the best way forward. The class teacher however insisted, and after all she was the professional and not me . So very reluctantly, I agreed we would give her approach a go.

The term had started in the second week in September, and despite our best efforts, our son spiralled downwards into a deep depression. He felt that they hated him, and that they were permanently telling him off. Our son started to have emotional outbursts in the school and tried to hurt himself by throwing himself down a set of six stairs. The school did not know how to react, so they called me. For the first six weeks of his secondary school life, I received a telephone call from them daily. Our son would be waiting for me, in the square that connected the school, on a bench, sobbing. He hurt his back quite badly, he was bruised as if he had had a car accident or something similar. Each day when I got to school he would run into my arms sobbing, begging me to take him home, and never bring him back. My husband and I had decided that in the first parents evening in the seventh week of school we would have to get them to change everything. As far as we were concerned it was not working at all. Sadly I can tell you we never got to that parents evening. The next event was to change all our lives forever.

Our evenings in these six weeks were a misery for the entire family. Our older children would go quickly into their own rooms, out of the way, as fast as they could. Our youngest son would sit and sob, he would cry and cry. He would even shout loudly into my face, asking me why I was not listening to him. On some occasions he would just sit and stare around, not talking to anyone.

One evening, just as normal the entire family had vacated the living room of the house, my husband had gone to work, and the youngest sobbed talking to Dino the dog about his worries. Then, the house became quiet, too quiet. I do not know if it was a mothers instinct, or what it was, but I realised my son was not around and that the crying had ceased. I got up and walked through the kitchen/dining area out into the laundry room. There we had a second bathroom, similar to a wet room. This room had a toilet, sink and shower. The shower had a curtain which ran on a stainless steel rod from the roof. My son had attempted to hang himself from the steel rod via the curtain. He was suspended in the air, with the curtain wrapped several times tightly around his neck. I screamed very loudly and grabbed at my son, taking his weight, as I tried to get him down he was crying at me to leave him to die. He was never going back to that school.

As parents we had faced many things in our lives, but, I cannot explain actually in words how we felt. If you have a child, and that child is so sad,at any age, but at the age of eleven years old, that he would attempt to take his own life, rather than go to school again. I can tell you that, in your head a voice is screaming, ' its enough already'. That night I cuddled my son, in my arms, throughout the night, we cried together. I vowed to him I would make it right for him somehow. We rang the school the next day and told them our son was ill and would not be coming back to their school.

I tried to keep as calm as possible, in a situation where my whole body was working on autopilot. The next day I rang the clinical psychologist and told her what had happened. She advised me to take him to our local GP, to one who knew him well. She would talk to the paediatrician, and would make an appointment to see our soon as soon as she could. She told me not to take him to school again at this time. When we called to see the GP, he was absolutely amazing. He had hardly ever seen our son, as he was never ill, (that seems such a strange thing to say). What I mean to say is that, he never got colds, tummy upsets, the measles, nothing. It was just as well as he had enough to cope with. The GP looked at me with very wide eyes, as, crying very quietly, I told him what my son had done to himself the previous evening. I told the GP why he had done it, and I told him what the psychologist had said that morning. The GP sat back in his chair and looked at my son carefully. My son told him very articulately, "he did not need a doctor, he simply needed never to go to school again". The doctor advised us he needed time to think about the situation, he explained to my son, that he had a full surgery of sick people outside his office, but that he would like to discuss the matter further with him, if that would be OK. The doctor agreed with my son and stated it was a good idea, to actually have a break from school at this time. He made an appointment for us to see him in the evening surgery two days later, he advised us he would clear four appointments so that we could have the time to talk. My son liked him, he had spoken to him as if he was grown up and not like a stupid child. He had also told him he needed to take time off school, so this was what he wanted to hear.

At the evening appointment with the GP, it became clear that he had spoken to the clinical psychologist and the paediatrician. He told our son he had depression, severe depression and that he thought he ought to take some medication for this. My son asked "what kind of medication?", and the GP said, that for children there were only a couple of drugs that were suitable, that in order to take them we would have to see a a psychiatric consultant. He advised us that for children with such difficulties it was often the case that some form of medication was needed. He had spoken to the people involved and had been advised to prescribe a drug, an antidepressant. My son objected and said he would not take any drug, and especially not one that was addictive. I knew that it would have to be his decision, my son had been through enough and I was not about to force feed him drugs. We left the doctors surgery, the doctor telling me quietly that he would always be there, I simply had to call. I thought this was wonderful, my son certainly had some nice professionals on his side.

My husband was concerned also, he did not like the idea of any children taking such drugs, but knew we had to change , some of our sons black view point of the world. The days went on, our son was seen by all the doctors and the clinical psychologist saw him every week for a while. When our son saw the new paediatric psychiatrist, the man advised him he needed to try to see that the world was not such a dark place, and that at times, many people needed such drugs as antidepressants. Eventually at the age of twelve years old he agreed to take the tablets.

I believe the tablets did help at this time, but our son does not agree with this statement as he thought they made him feel funny, sick and a little spaced out. But, actually he was already being sick, daily. He was having panic attacks when we went out. He hated being around people, lots of noise and strange smells. If we went anywhere which was out of his immediate comfort zone he would have a panic attack. Those next few weeks were very hard on us all.

Our next thoughts were, 'what do we do now'. Well as these things happen, a small miracle was about to come our way . I have a friend who was a qualified teacher, had looked into doing extra education in order to help her teach the growing number of Dyslexic children she was coming across during her normal working days. During her research she had been in contact with the Dyslexia Association. She had visited one of their schools in the north west and she was bowled over at their fantastic approach to teaching and education. On one particular evening, when she called for a coffee, she talked enthusiastically about the school and the methods of teaching there. She urged us to go to the school and see for ourselves.

The next morning, our son was taken to his grandparents house, and my husband and I set off on the forty mile journey, to visit the dyslexia school.

DYSLEXIA NORTH WEST SCHOOL.

We drove along the motorway toward the dyslexia school which was in a small seaside town and we discussed what we now wanted from a school in order to meet our sons needs. We had no idea what the school was going to be like, or if in fact they would allow us to view the school unannounced. At this stage we had no preconceptions and in fact being honest we did not think there was a school that would be suitable for our son. We had visited many schools pre-secondary school and so we were fully prepared to be very disappointed.

As we drove along the sea front we came across a large Victorian property. This property looked as if it was an old folks home by the sea rather than a school. We parked the car and walked toward the main door. The door was locked and we rang the bell. A very tall gentleman came and and opened the door. My husband stated that we had a dyslexic son and asked if we could look around the school, and the man beckoned us inside. We were asked to wait for five minutes whilst he checked if someone was available to show us the school. A very nice young man came and introduced himself, he shook our hands, he was about 14 years old. He said he would be happy to take us around the school.

The school had a small lift and a large Victorian staircase which wound its way upward for several floors. We could hear the bustle of the classrooms as we walked by. This was clearly a school with a difference. We could hear laughter, chatting and classical music played on a tannoy system above our heads. We were shown into four classrooms where children of all age groups looked at us and then busied themselves with their activity's. Our wide open mouths must have shown on our faces, as we saw scenes inside the classrooms we had never seen before. Each classroom was a wide open plan space, there were no traditional desks placed in formal lines, but small purpose built desks, with high sides on them. The school called them corrals. Each room had a lovely view of the sea through several very large windows. The paint on the walls was soft and soothing, creating a friendly atmosphere within. There was also a large table of a spherical nature which was on wheels, these tables could higher and lower and children were seen, slightly sprawled, slightly leant across them drawing or writing. Some of the rooms had large bean bags in groups on the floor.

In the hall way there were lots of small computers. These we were advised were used by all the students daily. They were portable in nature, similar to lap tops but a little different. We were shown into a large kitchen and dining hall which was immaculate. We were told this was unused. Outside and to the back, there was a small yard area, which sported several basket ball portable hoops, of all heights. The tour of the school over, we were shown into a large staff room. We were advised the head was busy , but if we did not mind waiting, she would see us soon. We thanked the young man and he left us to our own thoughts.

My husband and I looked at each other and nodded in agreement. We both knew instinctively that this was the school we wanted for our son, there was no doubt in our minds at this point. We talked quietly together, and decided that we would tell the head teacher all about our son, we had not brought the paper information in the form of his educational statement with us. A nice couple entered the room, the man introduced himself as the head teacher and then hurriedly excused himself stating he had school business to deal with. We nodded toward him saying we were sorry we had come to the school unannounced. The lady who was very slight of build, smiled at us, shook our hands and introduced herself as a doctor, and also the second head of the school. She advised us that she did tests on individuals for dyslexia, and on the pupils in order to determine if they had improved or not.

We told her all about our son; the nursery school time, the junior school time and the secondary school time. I then told her very clearly what had happened and that at this stage our child had no school as far as we were concerned. We told her that we were unhappy with the way things had happened and that our son was in crisis. We painted a very truthful but black picture. The question she then asked us was, "what would you want for your son now?" I said that I wanted to forget education, to place the academics inside a dustbin and allow our child to be happy. To learn to like school; surely if a child is happy then he will learn. We stated we wanted our child to attend a school of this extraordinary calibre.

The doctor then took us on a second tour of the school, she advised us that all the details of the school had been devised with the dyslexic child in mind. The use of paint colours, the corrals, the uniform (which was comfortable) , the movable tables, the bean bags. She explained that most dyslexic children disliked crowds. For this reason the class numbers had been kept small, with no more than eight in a class. The classes had children of all age groups together. This was done on purpose, to have a small cross section of children. All the children had different abilities. All the teachers and teaching assistants had specialist special needs training. She also advised us that they had two other children who had dyspraxia at the school. We told her that at twelve years old our son and us had never met any other dyspraxic children . She stated that she thought that our son would fit in well at the school. With a maximum of forty five children at the school, places did not become available often.

She advised us of our next move forward, this was to send her our sons paperwork, and then to confront the education authority. For our son to attend this school we would need a statement of thirty five hours, as he would have to journey there by taxi and in this taxi he would have to be accompanied. The doctor told us she would advise them they had a place at the school for him, and we had to request the place. We thanked her over and over, we could not believe how lucky we had been in finding such a wonderful school. A school that looked to the whole child and not just academics.

When we arrived home, we happily told our son all about the school and to our delight he became very interested. He wanted to be with children that were like him, he wanted to meet other dyspraxic and dyslexic children. He no longer wanted to be so different. Maybe now he would have a chance to have friends. We wrote to the education authority with our request and waited patiently for their reply. The reply we got shocked us. They had said we could have any school we wanted at the age of eleven,but now at the age of twelve years old they turned our request down. They had never told us this school even existed. Actually our son could have attended this school from the age of four years old and we felt hurt and angry that he had not been given this opportunity. The emotional situation my son was in may never have occurred. We wrote to them again; we did not understand. Our son needed a school, not just any school, but this school, it was obvious to anyone he could not cope in a normal secondary school environment and we had never in this modern age heard of a child being twelve who could not even write his name. The dyslexia school had stated in writing that they had a place for him, and, that they believed he could achieve there. Unfortunately the education authority still refused our request. Time was marching on and we were afraid this place at this wonderful school would be filled with another child.

My husband and I drove to the education authority building, we demanded to see the higher manager, and within minutes we were shuttled into a side room. Two people came to see us, again we tried to state our case as level headedly as possible, but the higher manager simply stated that the decision had been made. My husband, (please forgive him) in sheer frustration for our sons plight, began to loose his temper, (my husband is one of the calmest people I know). This was our son and they simply refused point blank to listen. A security guard was brought to the room and we were escorted from the building.

During the drive home we both sat quietly and cried. Once again my husband and I were devastated. We could not understand their point of view at all, and they would not even listen to our point of view. This emotional roller-coaster we had ridden the last few years was becoming too much for us never mind our son. When we arrived home our son looked toward us as I tried in vain to smile at him. He cried looking at me, and he said, " look mummy, this is not like you, you have never been beaten, never, you will make it happen I know you will" . His faith in me was fantastic, but I did not share his thoughts.

My husband had to go to work and after hugging him goodnight I went to our room. I sat up all night trying to think of the one thing I had not thought of. The next morning I had devised a plan. This is what I did.

I rang the houses of parliament and asked to speak to my MP. I made an appointment to see him during his surgery that Friday morning, telling his assistant how urgent my situation was. When the Friday morning came, I went armed with all the paperwork we had. I was shown inside the large comfortable office, and I was introduced to my MP (for the very first time ever, I might add). I was advised that via telephone conferencing his office in the houses of parliament London were listening to us. The person there introduced himself. I told the MP as quickly and concisely as I could of my sons problems. I told them what my son had done to himself, I produced copies of all paperwork from the doctors, paediatricians, education authority and then I told him about the new school, the place we had been offered and the refusal of the education authority to help us. I stated we did not want to lose the place, I advised them of my sons IQ and told him of my sons inability to read and write anything. I finished by stating if my son did not get this place in this school, I feared what he may do next. I asked the simple question " please will you help me".

There was quiet in the room, and I looked toward this person who I had previously only seen on my television screen. He nodded, saying "leave it with me". He gave instructions for his people in London to get the Education minister on the phone. He shook my hand and said I would hear from him very soon.

Feeling unsure of what would happen next I drove back to our village. Forty eight hours later we received a telephone call from the education authority, advising us that they had looked again at our request and they were advising us that we could send our son to the dyslexia school. The school would contact us within the next day or so and the paper work would follow shortly afterwards. The thirty five hours had been approved.

The following day we were invited to the school with our son for his first visit; for him to meet them, and for him to meet some of the other children there. It was decided that he should start as soon as possible, and I would drive him to school and collect him in the evenings until he was more comfortable there. At a later date a taxi and a person to accompany him would be appointed. This would be arranged when the paperwork caught up with things. Our son loved the school, and told us that many of the children and the teachers were in fact very clever. This pleased him more than anything. All the children took packed lunches, thus the school was able to spend more of the money on the pupils and not expensive kitchen staff. We collected our sons new uniform, and drove home listening to our son chat about his new beginning.

The very next day I wrote a letter of thanks to my MP, and we will always be very grateful to him. I began to drive our son to and from school, praying for this placement to work for everyone. My prayers were answered and our son began to slowly fit into a school of youngsters just like him. For the first five weeks the school ,toe by toe, introduced some class work, and this approach worked well. Instead of overwhelming our son, everything was kept very low key at the beginning. Now please do not misunderstand me, he still took quite a while to settle into his new routine, things were not totally plain sailing. But, it was by far the best they had ever been and we all knew that.

If you have a child who is very dyslexic, who struggles with everything, who fails to fit into the box the educational authority wishes to place them in, my advise is to contact the dyslexia association. Visit their schools, and talk to their professionals. The teachers, and staff at this school we regard as the best ,most caring and knowledgeable people we have ever met. They, we believe, helped to change our sons perspective of the world. We will never, ever, be able to thank them enough. Our son at twenty one years of age , living in a different country is still in contact with some of the teachers he met at this school and he regularly asks their advise, even today.

THE DYSLEXIA SCHOOL, A NEW START.

At the age of twelve, as I said before our son could not read or write. After only a short time at the school he was making vast improvements; at the age of twelve and a half he was attempting to write. His writing resembled one long line of weird shaped letters. We were never able to decipher it, but the amazing thing about this strange writing was that our son knew exactly, what he had written. No one ever said; "NO, do that again". All that was said was, "that's very good, why don't you read it to me". We very quickly adopted this approach. As he attempted to do some homework for the very first time, or when he brought home a story he had written, that he was proud of. all members of the family would frustrate him a little as we asked, " please read it to me".

Within the school was a drama class, where the children acted out their frustrations. They also did sports at the local YMCA, or they did swimming lessons. At the age of thirteen our son swam for the very first time and gained his very first certificate. On this occasion we were so proud, words cannot say. I took him and bought him a gift as a well done celebration.

A few weeks after our son had started at the school the head master beckoned me into his room. I can tell you,that, stood before a head teacher, a mother had never been so worried, after all I had stood before many teachers with regard to my youngest son and what they said to me had never been good. I took a deep breath and prepared myself for the worst. The teacher smiled at me, he had seen that look before, many times. After all this was the school that gained all the children, normal (that word again) schools could not cope with. He began, " today, has been a remarkable day for your son, we are very proud of him, this is the first day he has not come to my office, to inform me, how cross he is with the other pupils in his class". I simply stared back at him, I did not really know what to say to such a statement. The head continued, " there is always a defining moment, that makes us as teachers, aware, when each child begins to settle into the school". "This is your sons moment, from today he will make progress". I remember this moment as if it was yesterday, I must have looked like an idiot, I stood shocked, and still, for a moment or two and then I moved forward and hugged the head teacher. " Thank you, thank you very very much" I said. I wanted to skip out of his room but I did in fact manage to compose myself enough to walk sensibly to my car.

The teacher was correct, from that day forward, our son made progress. He was appointed a lady who was to accompany him in the taxi, she was a lady of age and our son loved her. She was interesting, kind and with her help our son actually went to school alone for the first time in his life. Our son even liked the taxi driver. For a child with trust issues, this was true progress. Four months later they asked the same taxi driver to collect two other children as well, if I am honest our youngest did not react overly well to this information, but he did share the taxi with as little protest as was possible.

The next thing I am going to tell you about, seems strange even to us, you may not believe it but, I can assure you it is a true fact. The children at the school were always being encouraged to think of others, and, one of the people who visited the school regularly was a pastor who had a church in the small seaside town where the school is based. This pastor also sponsored an orphanage and school in Mexico. Within the school was a small group of students,who were Christians and who joined together to discus; bullies, parents, failing, helping others, raising money for the orphanage etc.. these children often helped with morning assemblies. Our son joined this group and made friends with one or two of the children. The children were visited by some university students from Canada. The students stayed in England for two months, and they were regular visitors to the school. On leaving the school, for the last time, these students put on a special assembly. At the end of the assembly they made a gift to the small Christian group, my son was a member of. Each child was given a Bible, not just your regular Bible, but a Bible for teenagers. The print was clear, and within the book all manor of teenage questions could be answered. Each Canadian student had written inside the cover of our sons book, these were special messages to him about never giving up, staying true to yourself, and how it had been a pleasure to be in his company. Over the next three months our son read the teenage bible, we do not quite know how. Did everything come together at this time for him ?, possibly. Was this because he was feeling happier at school ?, possibly. We do not know the answer, but at the age of thirteen our son began to read for the very first time in his life. This was a momentous occasion for him. From this day forward our son read all kinds of books, more of a factual nature, and generally about his interests. Do not misunderstand me, our son is still dyslexic, this means that in a restaurant, a menu containing fancy fonts, or perhaps if he is feeling under pressure, he will still be unable to read. This never goes away. If you are dyslexic, you simply are and will be for the rest of your life.

The school reminded the children every day, of the many famous people, they may have heard of, who were and are dyslexic. Thus installing in the children a sense of future.

Famous dyslexic people include; Tom Cruise, Cher, Orlando Bloom, Walt Disney, Pablo Picasso, General George Patton, Thomas Edison, Sir Richard Branson, and Steve Jobs (the founder of apple computers). The list is extensive, many people admit to being dyslexic today but not so many are keen to admit to being dyspraxic. Being dyspraxic carries a larger stigma, however some very famous dyspraxic people are; Sir David Bailey, Sir Richard Branson, The son of the famous singer 'Sting', and most famous of all today Daniel Radcliffe (the young actor who played Harry Potter).

All the children were asked daily, ' what are you going to be when you grow up'. It is a difficult question to answer when you fail at most everything you do, the children just concentrate on ' today', but the question was repeated and repeated.

The next event, for me, shows the unique difference in this school. The head teacher played classical music daily to the children, by means of an overhead tannoy system. The belief behind this is that classical music helps a child to concentrate more and helps with their overall IQ. The children however, like most children do not agree with the teacher. On one occasion, the children joined together and hijacked the school tannoy system. They played their own choice of music for the whole school to hear. The head teacher however was not angry, no, on the contrary, he was very pleased. He gave all the children involved class points for their initiative. He also made an agreement with the pupils that the class gaining the most points weekly, for work and good behaviour, would be allowed to chose a CD to play once a week. His only request was that the music was not a heavy metal band. We thought this was amazing.

The school constantly gave rewards to the children for honest, good behaviour and hard work. For finishing work early they could play a game, go on a computer or play snooker. The head teacher had the extreme idea to divide the school car park in half. In one half of the car park he then built a half pipe for skate boards and roller blades. He allowed all the children to play on this if they received good comments from their teachers.

LIFE AT HOME FROM 12-15 YEARS.

I recently watched a program about a famous person who told the nation during a TV documentary how difficult it was for them growing up, at school, and the struggle they had being dyslexic. The reason I have chosen to write this book is to show that the struggle is not just that of the child but of the whole family, of the schools to provide help, of the teachers and the doctors. People must understand that being dyslexic and dyspraxic is not just about reading and writing, it is about coping with every day events and peoples attitudes to them as individuals.

After our son had tried to take his life, things at home changed. Not going back to the secondary school was the first huge change, and of course, this meant me, being at home with our son. My husband continued to work nights, but he increased these nights in order for me to be off work with our son. Thus trying to make up for the loss of income. At first we lived our life between doctors appointments, seeing first this person and then the other. Our son did not settle to sleep at night either, nor did he enjoy his normal routine of watching the open university. If he did sleep, he would wake up screaming, I was never able to console him. He would talk to me in gibberish, and get angry at me when I just could not understand what he was trying to say. Every night was the same, the pattern of events was beginning to make me exhausted. The psychiatrist said that they called his screaming in the night 'night terrors'. He told us that this was very common amongst children who had suffered a traumatic event. He also told us that dyspraxia was a strange disorder, that not only did it affect fine and gross motor skills but it was possible to be verbally dyspraxic. Verbal dyspraxia may take many forms, from a total mix up of the language, to putting words or sentences back to front. He believed that during our sons night terrors he was so traumatised that he was verbally dyspraxic .

After our son agreed to take the antidepressant medication, and the hospital appointments became a little less frequent, we decided that we should have some kind of firm plan for the future. But, this was easier said than done. We were all emotionally spent by the recent events, no one more so than our son. Our older sons lived away from home at this stage, which for their sakes we were glad of.

People do not realise that when a child has problems within a family unit, the other children in the family suffer to. When one child takes up so much of the parents time, even though they as his siblings try to understand the situation, they resent him, just the same for getting so much attention. This is human nature.

One evening, over a bottle of red wine my husband posed the question, "perhaps we all need a holiday, a holiday with a difference, a total change of scene ?". I did like the idea, but this was November, and everywhere was cold or raining. We had our son to think of, how would he cope?. We always went camping, but camping in November did not appeal to me at all. We talked it over for days, eventually deciding that if we chose a holiday that would be appealing to our son, he may relax a little and enjoy it. So, with this in mind we looked at a winter sun holiday, we decided on 'The Gambia'. We had never been before, the furthest we had been on an aeroplane was to Spain to visit Grandparents.

The next day I got myself busy planning a holiday, a holiday that would entertain a very bright young man. I booked us into a large Motel complex, I booked a five star family room with air-conditioning. We actually did not plan to spend very much time there, but it was decided it would be a good idea to have a good base to come back to, if things became difficult. Then I planned activities, trips to here, there, guides, transport, drivers and a stay in the bush in a small Gambian village. The decision was to make the holiday so busy and interesting that we would need a holiday when we came home.

Our plane tickets in hand we drove to the airport, for the long journey to The Gambia. I was so worried this decision would backfire on us, I found it very difficult to settle. My husband, bless him slept the entire plane journey, working permanent nights can be most difficult when you have to make the change to daytime living. Our son watched films on TV screens and slept the rest of the journey. When the plane touched down, and we exited, we had to walk across an old air strip into a customs area. When the passports were stamped we caught a coach to our Motel. The journey on the coach was difficult as we were all hot, and, it took about two and a half hours until we arrived at our destination. After checking in we were taken across some gardens to our family room. The first thing our son did was to open the thick curtains to the balcony and look at the surroundings.

We went down into the main motel to get some food from the restaurant and our son suddenly developed an independence we had not witnessed before. He collected a plate and proceeded to pile this plate as high as he could with fruit. All the staff at the motel were staring at us, and more so, at our son, we could not understand why. Soon however it became evident this was because he has white blonde hair, all the Gambian nation have dark hair and for most of them, it was the first time they had seen such blond hair on anyone. The staff were asking him if they could touch his hair. Now this was a young man who hates to be touched, and I mean hates. It took him years to accept a cuddle from his grandparents, so we were instantly concerned as to how he would react. He was a little uncomfortable but he allowed them all to feel his hair. This was his first positive moment in months.

That evening we walked quietly by the edge of the sea, many Gambian people were walking at a distance from us simply staring in our direction. I did feel a little uncomfortable, but surprisingly our son did not. The next morning, as we walked outside, we passed a window with a fly screen attached to it. Stuck on the fly screen were several large flying insects. Our son stopped and began to free all the insects that were stuck fast on the screen, from several locusts, to praying mantises. He would not go to the restaurant until he had set them all free. We continued on our way and left him to be alone with the insects. He eventually, came for breakfast, which for him was a very large plate of fruit. We went straight on our first trip which saw us journeying around Gambia looking at their tourist sights. A local fish farm, a carpet factory and lastly a school. At the school our son stared in amazement. The walls were concrete and unpainted, the children had no pens, pencils, books, games, nothing. Our son amazed us with his next statements, as he began to tell the other holiday makers, in our party, information about Gambia. He stated that from that year, the minister for Gambia had declared that all children should go to school, and be given a uniform, this one uniform was to enable the children to all look alike, but it had to last their school lives. Some children were having to walk many miles each day to the nearest school, through rough country, on simple roads. The tourist guide nodded toward him, and our son began to gain the respect of the entire party.

When the excursion was at an end we were taken back to the motel. Our son went into the gardens and laid out on the floor. He stayed perfectly still for the longest time we have ever seen. He did this to allow all the insects to crawl on him, he thought they were fantastic. It was a sight I will never forget. Later that evening as we walked by the sea, we came across some Gambian women, who marvelled at our sons hair, he allowed them to touch his hair and then to braid it which was a very amusing sight. My husband paid the fee, and because the ladies had no change they asked us if we would accept a watermelon instead of money. My husband agreed, so we went on our way watermelon in hand. Now, what are we to do with this? My husband asked. "I know", our son said. He then talked at great length about the Gambian people, and of how if your father was a chef, you as the son had to be a chef. If your father is a fisherman, you must become a fisherman. We thought this was all well and good, but we still had a watermelon in our hands, and a restaurant with more fruit than we could possibly eat. When we arrived at the Motel our son grabbed the watermelon and set off at the run into the gardens, my husband motioned to me, to leave him be, to do whatever he was going to do.

Our son actually went into the gardens and approached the head gardener who was eighty two years old. He gave the watermelon to him and ran back to the restaurant. After his obligatory very large plate of fruit he walked back toward the gardens to explore the large spiders there. He soon came back to join us, carrying a two foot long seed pod; it transpired that this was a dried seed pod, given to him as a gift from the head gardener. These seed pods are musical instruments in Gambia. Our son has this seed pod today as part of his musical instrument collection.

Our next journey was our longest and most exciting yet. We met our driver and guide and the three of us climbed into a kind of small people carrier that had seen better days. We then journeyed hundreds of miles deep into the bush. This journey took the best part of the day. Our guide chatted to our son about all manor of things relating to Gambia. When we arrived at our destination, it was a small collection of mud and twig huts called ' a compound '. We were shown to our family hut, which had mosquito nets over simple beds. We then went to a communal hut to eat. That evening, we joined our guide and climbed inside a large dug out canoe. We then paddled quietly across the Gambian river as the sun was setting. We went in and around the mangroves which lie in the middle of the river. The journey was wonderful and our son was mesmerised at the wildlife that came alive at night. The colourful birds, snakes, large iguanas, and the absolute quiet was almost deafening. It was a journey to last a few hours and it was a lovely experience. When we returned to the shore our son sat amongst a colony of mud-skippers, we looked at his happy face and felt blessed.

Our next journey took us further into the bush to visit a school there. In this school the head teacher talked about his greatest problem being snakes. These snakes would slither into his classrooms and of course, some of them were very dangerous. The school was similar to the other one, plain, no paint, no posters, no books. But our son made an observation that all the children were very happy there. He told the teachers how many children in Britain were very unhappy at school and that he wished that all the children were as happy as the Gambian ones. As our son made this comment, I felt a lump rise in my throat. The head teacher looked very amused by this statement and he asked if the children could sing for us. The children did sing to us and we all left feeling very happy, and just slightly guilty for having so many possessions at home. That evening during our meal, our son chatted happily about the insects, the bats, the snakes at the school and pondered what our next day would bring.

The next day saw us journeying into a small town with our guide and driver. We climbed out of the car and walked around some market stalls which were full of recycled goods, jars, tins, paper etc.....We were on our way to visit a headman, who had his own compound and as such, he looked after six other adults and around fourteen children of various ages. My husband stated to the driver that we should actually take a gift for the family with us. It was agreed that this gift be a useful one, so we bought some sugar, candles, matches, soap and pens. Our son purchased a bag of lollipops, which were also whistles. When we arrived at the compound the head man showed us around his crops, his rice store and his collection of small buildings. Our son looked on in horror as he saw that the family owned three beds, so some would be lucky to share a bed, but the rest of the family slept on the floor. Our son presented our gift to the head man, and then he gave each child a lollipop. The children actually took the gift and stared at our son. He looked on exasperated, until I whispered to him, it was possible the children had never had a lollipop before. My son nodded and held out a lolly and proceeded to unwrap it slowly and then place it in his mouth with the noise mmm..... as he watched all the children copy him, he was actually chuckling to himself, a sound we had not heard since he was five. He then turned the stick over and blew lightly into it. A small whistle sound emitted from it, sending all the children into fits of laughter including our son. My husband and I exchanged a glance, and both of us were quietly crying, at the sight of our son laughing out loud. I wished silently that I could bottle that moment.

The next day saw us journeying back toward the motel, the driver explained that all his family lived in a small village along the way and that he had not seen them for nearly four months. My husband insisted that he stop the vehicle and spend some time with his family. Again the moment was very touching indeed, as we watched almost sixty family members running, and laughing as they embraced our driver. They gave us a drink of coca cola and soon we continued on the journey.

When we arrived at the motel, my husband gave the two men a very large tip indeed. To a northern European this was not really a vast amount of money, but in Africa it was everything. This tip was equivalent to two years salary each. The tip, shocked them but, it was not just because they had been wonderful at their jobs, and not because we had enjoyed the experience, but because of the moments of absolute joy we had shared as parents, as we had watched our son be happy for the first time in years.

As we sat and ate our large plates of fruit that evening, we were joined by some of the other holiday makers. They asked us about our experiences and we heard our son excitedly telling them of our adventures. To our delight one of the women had collected some beetles for our son and as she gave them to him she said, " I collected these for you because I knew you would be able to tell us all about them, none of us have ever seen them before". Our son accepted the beetles and began telling her about them, feeding habits, habitats etc.. Was it actually possible that other people looked at our son and saw a wonderful intelligent boy, just as we did !!. We were very happy indeed, these were feelings, even we, as parents had forgotten how to experience for a long time.

The next day we took a large ferry boat for a relaxing journey up the Gambia river, on board we shared a meal with other holiday makers. It was a very nice trip. With each journey and new experience our son physically relaxed before our eyes. The evenings were spent in the same way, a walk along the sea shore and then a meal of as much fruit as we could eat. Some evenings there was music and other evenings we simply sat by the pool looking at the stars.

The next day my husband and son had a trip together. They were to go sea fishing. They spent the whole day together and when they came back to the motel our son chatted happily about the experience, what they had seen and the people they had met.

This was to be the final trip as the next day we had to go home. In the morning as we packed and made our way to the coach, we were all very quiet. It was for all of us a time of reflection and we felt very sad as we knew soon, we would be home again. As a family we will remember this holiday forever.

When we arrived home, we did see a change in our son. It was a change that I find a little hard to describe in words, but perhaps it is better to say he was a little calmer in himself. We changed our routine and each evening, after my husband left for work, my son and I would take a sort of picnic upstairs. We would sit on my bed, and watch some documentary or another. We would have long discussions about the world, nature, politics, etc.... He would talk of a future when he was grown up and of how he would make clean, safe power for Europe in the deserts and of how he would take water to the people who had none. As we had no school, our days were spent in museums, stately homes anything in fact that we could learn about, and that was nearby.

When you have a child with special needs, people do not realise but this affects all aspects of your life. In our nearby market town was our family dentist. As the children had grown, I had taken them to the dentist often. For our youngest, as he was always so healthy and ate no sweets, the visits to the dentist were simple ones. The dentist would sit him in the chair and simply check his teeth, give him a sticker for his coat and we would leave. On one of these visits, the dentist found a small cavity. He advised me of this fact and I asked "when was he going to fill the cavity, would this be today or a future appointment". The dentist then shocked me by saying, "he could not fill the cavity , we would have to attend the clinic of a special needs dentist". I felt a little thick now because I firstly did not know these dentists existed, and secondly did not understand why the family dentist had not told me this earlier. Why had I brought a child, with deep trust issues, to a dentist for years, to build up some trust, when he was not prepared to actually be a dentist to that child.

So, armed with a telephone number of a dental surgery for special needs children, we went on our way. At home I rang the surgery, I explained the situation and they quickly made us an appointment. I should not have worried because I can tell you they were quite simply brilliant. They saw our son regularly after that moment. When our son reached the age of thirteen we were sent to a dental surgeon at the hospital. This gentleman was also brilliant, our son liked him a lot. He had large posters of the rain forest on his ceilings and was very interesting. He designed a brace for our sons jaw, and stated that if he wore it every day, it would eventually move his lower jaw outwards, thus giving him a slightly larger chin. Our son hated his looks and had at times, in his life, become a little over obsessed with his chubby cheeks. (which were a genetic feature, shared by some members of the family) This brace was never taken off, and eight months later our son had a very chiselled, handsome, new look.

Another dislike of our sons was of smells, he would never go into a market hall because he said it smelt very bad indeed. He would never sit in a restaurant because he would say it smelt of the dead flesh some of the other customers were eating, in the form of a steak or chops. He would never go to a hairdressers as these places were filled with smells and lots of other people. At times our son has had quite long hair, and over the years he has had many styles. I have taught myself to cut his hair. I still cut his hair today and twenty one years later I don't do such a bad job, either.

When our son started at the dyslexia school we decided to purchase a motor home. This purchase was made in order for us to have many family holidays, of a relaxing nature. We went on many holidays to France where our middle son worked. We travelled around France for six weeks at a time, (owing to the fact that my husband saved all his holidays and bank holidays up and used them together). Our son would spend day after day body boarding in the waves of the atlantic ocean. Even though his swimming resembled a doggy paddle, he showed no fear and persevered with his new learnt sport. On one such holiday, whilst on a beach in the south west of France our son was to stumble across another activity. As my husband and I sat watching the ocean in front of us, our son called out to us. We turned around toward the sound of his voice and to our amazement he was stood on the top of an extremely high wall. My husband told him off for wandering away from us, and asked him to walk around the wall and back to us. He did as he was told, and was soon by our sides. He then explained that he had climbed up to the top of the wall. We were very shocked, and told him it was a silly thing to do as he could have been very hurt, was he to have fallen. Five minutes later, he disobeyed us and was again climbing the very high wall. My husband motioned for me not to shout, as that action alone could indeed find him falling. We both stood mesmerized, watching this child who had visual physical motor control difficulties, and a visual body tremor, scale the wall like a monkey. He quickly found his way to the top. He then scaled this wall over and over again, possibly over twenty times. We made an agreement with him, that if he did not take such risks again, my husband would take him to a local sports centre, that had a climbing wall and that they would both learn to climb safely and properly, using ropes and harnesses etc....Now at the age of twenty one, our son is a fantastic climber. On one occasion, my husband

and son, used their equipment of ropes, pulleys and crampons, to help a tree surgeon fell a very large and dangerous tree.

We purchased a small sailing yacht called a 'Lazar pique'. My husband would pull this small yacht behind the motor home. The journey would be to the sea in nearby Wales, or to a lake in the Lake district. My husband spent hour after hour teaching our son about ropes, knots, and sailing. They loved these times and together they developed a whole new love for the sea, and found a hobby that our son could succeed at.

Yes it was still true that our son still hated to be touched, he still hated smells, he still used only a fork to eat and he still spent days before school terms began, and weekends in panic because of the forthcoming school days. But, we did try everything in order to help him achieve something, and have hobbies he could tell his peers about. He still had obsessions, these obsessions changed to different things as he got older. At this stage in his young life, one such obsession was about the cleanliness, of at first the school toilets and later any other public toilet. He would make himself ill throughout the day by refusing to enter the room, just in case he may come into contact with any germs. I tackled this strange obsession by purchasing many fine pairs of latex gloves, he could carry with him anywhere. After these purchases, he would use the toilets and then he would throw the gloves away after exiting the facilities. Armed with these gloves his life went quietly back to normal (that word again).

Our son continued to grow very tall indeed, he always looked older than his peers simply because he stood head and shoulders higher than any of them.

He continued to go to the boys brigade when we were at home, and continued his love of animals.

He has always had a keen interest in history, but this interest became a deeper one. His knowledge of the smallest details would never cease to amaze us all. On some occasions, he would even challenge the history teacher at school. Unfortunately, or fortunately depending on your perspective, he would often prove beyond all doubt, that in fact, his fact, was the correct one. This at times made for some very difficult situations.

However, our son via tape books, videos and then DVD's, En-carter (on the computer), television, the internet, encyclopaedias, magazines, in fact by any means possible, continued to soak up any knowledge he could.

He had however, no organisation skills at all, nor does he have today. What is the saying ?, 'he would probably be late for his own funeral'. Trying to organise himself has to be a way of life.

His writing is still very dyslexic when he is tired but it can be better on some occasions.

From the age of twelve to fifteen years of age, he still had no friends at all at home and this had started to bother him deeply. It also bothered him that people would watch him walking on the balls of his feet, as he always had done, but as he became older, people would comment or snigger asking, " why did he walk like that?".

Some friends of ours once came to our home for a meal and the couple asked my husband, "why our sons hands shook so much, and why did he become so nervous when he did anything?".

It seems a silly thing to say but all these things are true, you can spot a dyspraxic child or adult at fifty paces, by the very fact they walk on their tiptoes or the balls of their feet. It is also a fact that most dyspraxic people have seemingly, almost bendy fingers, that sometimes tremor as they concentrate on a task. But to our family he is just our son.

Another saying is "warts and all", well we do not see the warts, we only see the ALL.

ANOTHER CRISIS LOOMS.

School life proceeded without as many problems as there had been in the past, but, it was still like being on an emotional roller coaster. Our sons inability to react well to change was one of the biggest problems we had.

At the end of each term, the school had a policy, where the head teacher would mix the children up again into different groups, they would all begin the next term with a different set of children and a different class teacher. This policy was brought about because non of these children can cope with change, the idea is that change happens all the time, and if it happens often enough they may become used to it.

For our son each change of class teacher was a severe problem, he would spend three to four months just getting used to the new teacher. During this time he would cry persistently, because he would believe the teacher hated him. This black view of the new person in his school life was very hard to change.

The new children would also pose problems, some of the children in the classroom would behave quite badly at times, their constant struggles, would lead to frustrations. Some children internalise these frustrations, but others become very destructive, both to each other and school property. Our son would find this very difficult to cope with. He would become very frightened of attending school and again he would feel that these children hated him. Everyone worked very hard with our son in an attempt to change his dark perspective of the situation, parents, teachers and clinical psychologist alike, but it was almost impossible to achieve.

However on the plus side our son was doing very well indeed with his reading, he now had a reading age that was almost equivalent to that of his age. His ability to see numbers was improving also. Both these improvements coupled with his intelligence meant that he was doing incredibly well, with the education side of things.

When a child has specific learning difficulties normally the child does not take GCSE's, they take examinations in small steps. These steps are called AQA's. They are in fact, small portions of the usual exams, broken into a possible twenty steps. When a child leaves a special needs school possibly they could have forty, or fifty AQA's. When there is a child with intelligence it is even possible they could have more.

Recognizing our sons potential, the teachers believed that he should take GCSE's. They kept telling him how bright he was, how he would be their star pupil. How it was his duty to show the other children at the school, that with hard work everyone can achieve. In the past, the school had a child go on to the local college , to study Art. They had placed his information in a picture frame, on the wall of the hallway for the whole school to see, as they were very proud of this fact. As a parent of the school I was proud for them.

This is the point where our problems began to spiral out of control. Our son actually knows he is very clever, he has known this from a very young age. Many of his frustrations came from the fact that his physical ability's, and his emotional ability's have never been at the same level as his intelligence. He also has a problem with people who are not so intelligent as he is, he continually admits 'he does not suffer fools gladly'.

At the age of fifteen the school seemed to believe that he would cope well with the possibility of doing examinations. They gave him old papers to complete in sections and he began doing AQA's at the same time. They talked to him about college or university.

The result of all this talk, for him was that he had a breakdown at home, he became very upset begging us to tell the school he needed to stay their until he was nineteen. This was a possibility for some children, but the head teacher thought the education authority would want our son in a college as his academics were improving so greatly. The problem was that his emotional state was plummeting simply with the idea of change.

We made an appointment to see first his class teacher, who seemed to treat us like over anxious parents. This did not bother us, I am sure all parents have been treated this way at some time in their children's lives. We then called to see the head teachers, they told us that our son was more than capable academically. We agreed, we were sure he was capable of this and much more. However, we stressed to them our sons anxiousness. They said all the children panic a little at these times, but after a while, with their softly softly approach, they all calm down. We had to trust in them, as they had indeed done wonders to help our son. So far they had achieved where others had failed.

Things at home however got far worse. Our son never slept, he tried to keep himself awake fearing his nightmares. This meant that at school he would fall asleep daily. He also became very clumsy, or I should actually say, clumsier than usual. His sickness reappeared in the mornings making it almost impossible to have breakfast. Because he continually felt sick, he could not eat and he began to dramatically loose weight.

Once again I met with the school and told them what home life was now like. I actually begged them to stop doing any GCSE work or papers with our son. I told them we, as parents did not care about the academics.

They said they would tread a little more gently in the future, that they were sure things would settle down.

A week later I received a telephone call asking me to go to the school. They said our son had been a naughty boy, and they would like to talk to me about it. I was shocked at this news. I have three sons and boys will be boys, but this child was never naughty. He would internalise everything, he would make everything his fault, he always blamed himself and would even hurt himself, rather than hurt others. At the school the teacher told me how a boy in the class had upset our son in some way. Our son then supposedly screamed in the classroom and pinned the child to the floor. My son sat there, he looked straight at me and told me he had done this because the boy would not stop annoying him. He had pinned the boy to the floor, to prevent him moving until the teacher arrived. I told him, what he already knew, that this was not the correct way to behave. I thanked the staff and left the school. I then asked myself, was this a more normal reaction for a boy of fifteen, or, was this reaction so out of character I should worry?.

My husband and I looked long and hard at the situation before us. Once again our son was drastically changing before our eyes and we felt powerless to help. The school continued to prime him for his GCSE's, and he continued to do AQA work. He hardly ever ate, he hardly slept and he had started to get severe panic attacks. He even got a panic attack in church and this was a place in which he felt happy and safe. He would have a panic attack in the car or when we went shopping, and the severity of these attacks seemed to be increasing.

Then one evening, before my husband went to work our son advised us that another teenager who was taking the same antidepressant drug as his, had taken his own life. He showed us the news story and he stated he would no longer take the medication. Fearing further problems if we stopped the drug, I rang the GP, who advised me that the report was true. A study had been completed, and, it had revealed that often this drug was responsible for creating feelings of suicide. I was speechless as this was the reason we were giving our son the drug in the first place. He advised me to think about reducing the tablets. He thought our sons history meant that he should not be on these tablets anymore.

I talked with my son for hours and the conclusion we came to ,was that, from the very next day, he would not take another tablet. This was not the way the GP had advised us to do it, but our son insisted he no longer wished to take them. He understood that the withdrawal would be difficult, but this was what he wanted. The following day I rang the school and stated he was ill with flu, and I would keep him at home until he was better. The next few days showed a strength in our son we had not seen before. He was very ill indeed, shaking, sick, headaches and very very sad . He cried and cried but he never took another tablet.

Here is the moment that shook our world,....

Our son advised us that he did not need a tablet to make him contemplate the ending of his life as he thought about this often, especially when people in his life would not listen to him. He did not want to take GCSE's, he did not want to go to college. He felt very frightened now and he said he thought about ending his life often to make his misery end. He said he felt very lonely and stupid, he was terrified of going to sleep because he could not stop thinking. He knew it was wrong, but he thought taking his life would make all the misery stop. He begged us to help him make his nightmare of a life end. He sobbed and sobbed and he looked at us with a despair that I have found hard to describe in words. We all hugged and cried together, our child shaking violently with each tear

As long as we live my husband and I will never forget that moment. That moment was a defining moment for us as parents, and we knew that if we wanted to keep our son, we had to show him we were listening to his pain.

A BRAVE DECISION.

The question we mulled over and over was, what can we do now ? We knew we had to do something and quickly, it seemed very difficult, as we thought, we had already done everything we could possibly do.

One evening after my husband had gone off to work, my son and I watched that evenings documentary in my room. I told him it was time for him to go to his room and he went off, promising to be quiet for the rest of the night. However I could not sleep, I was thinking so hard, my head hurt. Then an idea came to me, the idea was very radical, I did not know if it was possible, or if my husband would agree to it, but the more I thought about it, the more I was sure it could work.

When my husband came home the next morning, and our son was safely in the taxi, on his way to school. I sat down at the kitchen table and told my husband, I about my idea.

I made a cup of coffee and began. "I think we should sell the cottage and the cars and leave the country in the motor home", I said. Now what everyone reading this should understand, is that we were both over 40 years old. We were both born and bred in our small village in Lancashire. Our parents came from this village, My Father and my husbands mother were both born and bred in this village. Both our sets of parents were child hood friends. My parents had made a decision eight years ago, to live in Spain, for the better weather and a warmer retirement, but, my

SQUARE PEG ROUND HOLE

husbands parents still lived in the village. This was a very big idea for anyone to come up with, but for me it seemed huge.

My husband simply looked at me, sat back in his chair and thought. I went on, "well both our other sons are very well established now in their own careers". "One has his own place in a large town nearby and the other is living and working in France and has been for the last six years". "We will only be a plane ride away; anyway, the world is a small place today". "Many of our pets have died of old age, the only ones we have left is our large dog Dino, and a guinea pig and a chinchilla." "I could look into how we can take them abroad with us". "My idea is simply this, you cannot teach a clever child, to be clever, he simply is. However, what is the actual point of it all, if you are brighter than an encyclopaedia but, you are so scared of the world, you are to afraid to go to the local shop for a bag of sugar". "Surely, that is not correct". My husband still did not speak, he simply kept looking at me.

I continued, "You hate your job anyway, you hate working nights and this way we could all spend quality time together".(my husband had a very good job, he was an aerospace engineer) "I am sure if we place the house on the market it will take months to sell". "This gives us plenty of time to work out any details". "After we pay off the mortgage, the bills and the motor home loan, it is true, we will not have a lot of money, but, how much do we need anyway ? We will owe nothing to nobody." "We can take our son to all the places he has read about, we can take him to touch the things he has only seen in books". I was also thinking we could go to Normandy in France and take him to the beaches from world war two". "My husband was still staring at me, I thought that he thought, I had gone completely mad."

I continued, "We could look in France.... our son is happy in France, we could buy a property there, an old farm, raise animals, grow organic vegetables and fruit. You could have a workshop and make furniture and things". "We could do it, I am sure we could". "What have we got to loose?" "Lots of people make decisions like this every day, why not us"?

My husband continued to stare at me, then he said, "you do realise that this is the daftest idea you have ever had, let me go to bed, and think about it more."

My husband went off to bed, and I spent the whole day making a list, well two columns to be precise, on one list. The two columns were.. ' for and against ', a possible move away, somewhere ,I was very surprised myself that I had more in the column, ' for ' than against. I had convinced myself that it would work. I looked around our now beautifully renovated cottage, the renovations had taken seven years and lots of time and money. I looked outside at the rain, which was a constant where we lived.

What exactly is it all about anyway, we do all these things for our children, all parents do. However, if you have ever had a child that is so sad, they are unable to cope with the world, then I am sure nothing is worth anything, any more. Everything you have ever worked for in life looses its value. It does not matter where you live, how many TV sets you have, how large a garden you have, or which school your child attends. All these things are for your family, if you loose that, you have lost everything. No one had listened to me or my husband, not really !. The education department had waited until things were critical before they had acted, and then they were pushed to act. What, price would we pay, if we did not act, and act now.

Later that afternoon, my husband rose from his sleep early. Saying he was unable to sleep, he could not stop thinking about what I had said. Half an hour passed and our son came home in the taxi, he looked pale and stated he was feeling very sick. He told us, he had done a test that day, and he had decided to fail the test on purpose. He had decided this was the way to stay at the dyslexia school. If he failed everything, they would stop making him take exams and let him be. He started to cry, and sobbed louder saying, he did not want to go to a strange college. He said he could not talk to us any more he felt far to sick, he would go to his room and cuddle the dog.

My husband watched him go upstairs to his room and then said, "OK we will do it". "Tomorrow go to the local market town and place the house up for sale", "This evening I will enquire how much notice I am required to give at work". "somehow we need to find out about taking the animals abroad, perhaps the local Veterinary can help us".

I have always loved my husband, but never more than at that moment. We both knew that his parents would be very sad when he told them we were leaving. We knew that my sister would be sad but supportive at the same time. However, we knew our other two sons would support our decision, our eldest son had always thought we were crazy listening to the education authority, when we knew our son better than anyone and therefore in his eyes, we knew what was best for him, not some stranger in an office. Our middle son thrived on adventure and travel, we were sure he would be very happy for us all.

The next day I did place our house on the market, not for a huge profit but for a fair price. The estate agent told me this way the house would sell quickly. They were not wrong either, after four very quick viewings, three of which were before the for sale sign was in the ground. The last lady to call, made an offer of the full asking price. Her only request was that she could have my mirrors and dressing table and that she could take possession in six weeks time. The next day she paid a full deposit to secure the purchase. That evening, my husband handed in his notice at work which had to be done one month before your last day of work. Luckily for us, he had some holiday time to come which halved the time he had to work. Two weeks later he left his job for good. His company were very nice, they offered him a five year career break if he wished, he declined their offer because he decided he would never go back.

When I took the dog to the vets, in order for him to have his examination for a pet passport, she advised me that he had in fact got cancer. She did not think that it was bothering him at that time, but she saw no reason to apply for a pet passport, as that document is only for pets coming and going in and out of the united kingdom. She told me that he was never coming back. I was very, very sad but I decided to keep this information quiet for a while. She actually helped me export our dog, out of the UK.

We had very naughtily decided that we would smuggle our guinea pig and chinchilla out of the country, hidden deep inside our motor home. Silly documents, for such small animals, were very costly. One week later, when I went to the cage of the chinchilla, he had died , he had died of old age. We all cried lots, and also one week after this our guinea pig died, leaving us left with one pet, our dog. I felt like it really was working out for the best in some strange way, as if it was all meant to be.

We gave our large items of furniture to the local Salvation army and to nearby neighbours. On the day of the sale, we simply awaited a call from the solicitor telling us that the money was in the bank, mortgage paid. Our items we decided we could never part with, pictures, boxes of family photographs and some instruments were safely tucked into the attic of my husbands parents. The motor home was packed and ready to go.

Our son remained at his school until the day of our departure, on this day I rang the school and said he was ill. I wrote several letters to the school teachers and local authority members, thanking them but advising them we were leaving the country. As we climbed into the motor home, I clutched the letters to the various people and these were posted in the ferry port as we waited at Dover to cross the channel.

These actions may have seemed strange to others, but neither ourselves or our son told the school or medical profession that we were leaving, until we were sure we had left, just in case the sale of the house fell through, or maybe our thoughts were we would tempt fate.

As we drove away from our village, exactly seven weeks after I had initially thought of the idea to leave the country, our thoughts were not of sadness, or of worry for the future that lay ahead. Our thoughts were calm and happy, even of excitement at the prospect of the vast journey we had before us. We did not stop to view England, we did not stop to call on family or friends. All our goodbyes had been said in the days prior to our departure. As we boarded the ferry in Dover, we had a group hug. We stood on the deck, watching England's green and pleasant land fade away into the distance. Thirty five minutes later, We stood on the deck of the ferry watching Calais in France grow nearer and nearer. After climbing back inside our motor home we drove through Calais and made our way to a place called La Touché. We had visited this town before and had always planned this to be our first stay. From this point forward we simply had no plans, none at all. We would sit together each evening and plan as a family what we would like to do the next day.

The question you may be asking yourself now is,' how did our son react to our decision to leave the country ?, and how did he react to us selling the house etc..?'. Well, quite simply he reacted well. When we told him we had decided to sell the house and go away in the motor home he was at first amazed, and then he amazed us both, by staring at us and laughing out loud. He said something to us which he says often, even today, (the local authority states all children with learning difficulties have in fact got ' special needs '. They think this terminology to be a nicer one.) Our son looked directly at us and said in a silly voice " is it cause you is Special." We all laughed and our son began to count down the days on his calendar, using a five bar gate system. His last few days at school became less fraught for him. If the school believed him to be settling to the idea of exams, they were very mistaken. He was more settled because he knew we were true to our word and that we were bringing all these years of horrible school life in England to an end. Our son slept, the whole five hour journey through England to Dover ferry port. He awoke for the trip on the ferry. He was not sad nor was he happy he was simply a little more at peace.

That evening in France La Touché, we went for our evening meal at a restaurant we had frequented previously on our holidays. We purchased a bottle of champagne and happily toasted our new life together. At the end of our meal we walked back to our motor home and once inside and ready for bed, I began to read out loud, the new novel we had bought for the journey, ' Harry Potter'. As I looked at my family eagerly awaiting the next chapter, with relaxed smiles on their faces, I knew in my heart that we had made the correct decision, and that there was no going back.

PART 3

LIFE ON THE ROAD IN A MOTOR HOME.

Life in a motor home is very different from that in a house. Everything becomes an important factor, things that you never gave thought to before. For example, conserving water, the water tanks are only so large and when its gone its gone, until the next time you may be able to fill up. It becomes incredible how you can wash and brush your teeth in a single sink of water. We became experts in conserving everything and experts on living in a small space. You would not believe how many meals you can construct in just one pan. After a family discussion in France we decide that we had been over generous with ourselves regarding the amount of stuff we actually needed. In a bid to make more space we constructed a list of things we had but did not need. On this list for example were four cups, as there were only three of us, we only needed three. Six glasses were on the list, as the cups could double as glasses. Three pans, cushions, shoes, clothes, throws, hair dryer, anything in fact which we felt in hindsight we had been overindulgent in keeping. After taking all these belongings from the motor home, we looked around our new living space and felt happier, almost as if we could breath the air better than before in our newly expanded space.

Our son settled quite well to his new life, sleeping an incredible amount of time, we decided to allow him as much time as he needed to adjust, so we simply let him be. After all this decision was for life not just for a two week holiday. His normal routine of being awake all night had to change, we had no television. We had purchased a 12 volt TV and DVD player prior to our departure, however my husband had wired them in to play

DVD's only. We talked to our son and it was agreed that a family film was an event we could share, as we could always think of better things to do with our time than watch TV. We had purchased lots of board games which previously were not a strong point with our son, the idea being that we spent quality time all of the time.

My husband actually found it the hardest to adjust from the constant busy life we had held, his problem, that each day was not mapped out for you. It is a very hard task, thinking all the time what should we do now ?, where should we go ?, what is our plan for today ?. When you sit at home and contemplate a long holiday, or even winning the lottery it is never hard to dream of all the things you would do and the places you would go. When you have the opportunity to do just that, reality is a very different thing. Routine is suddenly gone and nothing is easy to do. I myself found the lack of routine the hardest and also the feeling of being unsafe, especially at night. I observed my son who also became anxious about safety, possibly picking up on the fact that I was . The feeling of freedom was overwhelming at times especially in France. The vast open spaces, the seemingly unpopulated countryside and the never ending cold but sunny days. However blundering from day to day with no routine or direction was incorrect and it began to affect us all.

So sat in the fresh air, during a picnic, we made a long list of all the places we had wanted to see but had never had the chance to see before. We divided these places into areas and decided to drive back to northern France where our proper journey would begin. We had beaches, castles, cities, science museums, even places we had been to before but wanted to see again. The last place on the list was in southern France on the border to Spain, a small place called Gruissan Plage. It was also decided that we would spend simply as much time as we needed at any one place, if that was a week so be it. If after one day we felt we had had enough, we would move on to the next. The list became our structure for our time ahead.

A routine was harder to forge when on the one hand we wanted a more organic sort of a day. This would have suited us as parents , but not our son (dyspraxic/dyslexic) this would not work, I was extremely aware that routine of some degree was required. So our days became a little more structured, first we got up and had breakfast, we would then dress according to the day ahead, we drove or walked or cycled to our place of choice. We always had lunch at the motor home so that we could eat healthy and then we would go for a walk to explore, we would then go back to the motor home for evening meal. We would then go another walk and just prior to darkness we would head back to the motor home, change for bed and the evening would end usually with myself reading to everyone in the motor home. This routine was simple to follow but it gave us just enough structure to our days.

On the days when we moved to a new place of interest from our initial list, we would travel most of the journey in one, stopping for a picnic lunch and then climbing back into the motor home until we arrived at our new destination. At first our son would not sight sea on these journeys, he would sleep throughout, but over time he did stay awake for some of the journey. Then the next day would begin with our normal routine.

A very important factor for us as parents was that our son be able to progress, and that he be given the time needed to do so. But progress he must, we strongly believed that his horrible time at school had actually served to hold him back. It was our belief that this had been proven to us, because when he first went to the dyslexia school, he became more relaxed and therefore he made improvements. Our whole theory to his future was built on this simple hypothesis.

So the way forward for us was really a very simple one. We picked our enemies very carefully. I will explain....; we had a child that still failed at most things. 1, Dressing himself totally correctly, 2, He was very shy, 3, He was also very outspoken, 4, His social skills in most situations were terrible, 5, He could not eat with a knife and fork, 6, He was unable to choose between anything at all, even between one drink or another. He had forged his way on a computer and this had become his friend, he would spend hours daily at home on one of his four computers, but we had taken this away from him, along with his beloved night time TV. 7, His writing was still terrible and his reading was laboured, when stressed his reading was non existent. This may have been enough for the education authority but it was not enough for me. My dream was that he be able to read a menu in a restaurant or the contents of the motor magazines he loved so much. 8, He could ride a bike to a degree, but due to his sore legs (many dyspraxic children experience very sore joints) he would soon get very tired and simply stop. The list is endless, but I chose one thing only from this list. I did not care if it took him two hours to get ready in the morning, I did not care about eating with a knife and fork for example, but I did want him to progress, even if this was very slowly. So one thing was selected, this was the thing I would work on for as long as it took. The first thing I chose was....; quite simply how to choose between one thing or another. A skill we all use daily but take for granted. For our son this was a nightmare; which T shirt should I dress in today, which shoes should I choose, which breakfast cereal should I have this morning, what should we have for tea, what should I drink, do I wish to accompany my mum or my dad. Being in a supermarket and asking him to choose between one brand of apples to another could send him into a panic attack or fits of tears. But this was a skill I knew he could not avoid in his future. Our main goal for our son was for him to be able to be happy and then to be able to function in society.

Every day I would lay out two T shirts and ask, " which one do you wish to wear today ?" My son would say , " I do not know , you choose" I would say very quietly, "No, I chose my T shirt, you must choose yours." I would walk away. Thirty minutes later our son would still be looking at the T shirts in front of him. Then you would here, " dad, which T shirt should I wear ?" My husband would grin in his direction and say " I don't know son, you choose." This would go on and on for ages, But we were stronger than him, we did not move until he choose. One day he amused us both by placing both T shirts over his head. But, this decision was a decision of sorts so we simply let it be.

During a cycle ride on the many cycle paths that France has to offer, if we came to a fork in the road we would stop, we would look at our son and ask " which way should we go ?" our son would do anything to avoid choosing, even crying very loudly, asking " why should I have to choose?". I would simply and quietly answer, "because we must all learn to choose". We have spent many an hour sat at a simple junction in a cycle path, waiting for our son to choose our direction. Our son did learn, but this was not a quick lesson to learn it took until he was twenty years of age, and still today he knows he has a problem with choice. He will look in my direction, laugh and say " I know, I know, because we must all learn to choose." as I sit quietly saying nothing.

Our son did settle well to motor home living, he loved the quiet times we had as a family. We watched him grow very slowly from a child who would sit in front of a computer screen to a child who would spend hours upon hours wandering up and down the beaches with Dino. He learned to enjoy the outdoor life and he would fascinate us by playing for hours with dragon and damselflies. Our son is a great conversationalist and he would talk to us for hours telling us all the history of one castle or one region of France.

On one visit to a town in the west of France we parked our motor home in a long lay by, chosen for its good proximity to most of the towns amenities. When we returned to the motor home after our first walk of the day, we noticed our motor home had been joined by another one. We could hear the most awful clubbing type music coming from the inside. I hate this sort of music as does my husband and son, but when the gentleman poked out his head saying hello, we were shocked to find the man was in his fifty's. This man was one of Britain's famous eccentric people. He was lovely, we spent the next few days listening to his wonderful colourful stories of his journeys in his motor home. He talked about the places he had been and the many people he had met. He talked directly to our son as if he was a young adult, he never questioned why we were on the road with our son, why he was not at school, he simply accepted that this was the way things were. When he left us to resume his journey, he shook our sons hand and said "the pleasure was all mine, how very interesting you are young man, I am sure you are headed for great things." As our son preened himself and quite rightly, I felt once again blessed that a complete stranger was able to see in our son what we could.

When we moved to the last town on our list we had arrived in the south of France. We drove around a little and then parked up on the marina in Gruissan Plage. This small town we had visited before on our holidays, we loved the area and felt quite at home here. As it was November the weather was turning very cold, our motor home was winterised but outside of the motor home we were very cold indeed. One morning when we awoke the mistral wind had began to blow, on this day we made popcorn and watched the epic film which was a favourite of mine, ' the Godfather '. Some hours later, we decide that we could not stay inside for days, so our son came up with the wonderful idea of journeying up the mountains to Andorra. The next morning, quite early we began the journey. We climbed ever upwards and as we got higher we came upon very bad clouds and some snow. We decided to stop in a small village for lunch, where amusingly for us, the entire inhabitants were running around shouting the French word for snow. We ate our lunch observing everyone running from door to door advising it inhabitants of the forthcoming dreaded snow. After lunch we continued on our journey, we were in hindsight a little foolish. Further up the mountains toward Andorra it became obvious just how foolish we were. Snow fell faster and thicker and we stopped to ponder just how silly we were being. The decision made, we turned the motor home around and headed back to Gruissan Plage. The next morning we decided it was simply too cold for us and as we had come from the north of England, we had simply had our fill of bad weather so, another decision made, we would head further south into Spain.

SPAIN A NEW BEGINNING.

During the past years our journeys to France were originally due to the fact that it was near to Britain and that both our older boys were studying French at school. Our youngest for a short time studied Italian, the dyslexic schools thinking behind this was that Italian is a sing song language and dyslexic children respond very well to rhythm. My husband and I went to terrible secondary modern schools, where no languages were taught at all. To enable us to get by in France, after our older sons stopped wanting to holiday with us, I took a course in French. I was not very good at first, but over time my confidence grew. Do not get me wrong I have never been neither shy or retiring but I do not have a good ear for languages, due to my inherited hard of hearing difficulties. It takes me most of my time with English, but with French, well lets just say we did our very best. Over time you do get used to the language, and the road signs etc..everything at least becomes more familiar than it used to be. When we visited Spain on holiday it was usually for one week with my parents. They lived in the Costa del sol. Our Spanish was non existent, not because we were lazy but our lives were so busy at home and in one week, yearly, you can just about learn to order a coffee and say thank you before its time to go home.

As we headed toward the Spanish boarder we regretted this fact deeply. The road was a toll road and you were obliged to take the appropriate lane for your vehicle. We selected the wrong lane and held up the traffic for one mile. At last a very unhappy man, climbed out of his snug booth and braved the winter chills, he helped us pay our toll and waved us on our way. We were all very shaken, this was a terrible start to our new beginning, in our new country. We drove deeper into Spain but our son kept saying, "I do not like this place, lets turn around." My husband kept trying to assure him that due to the bad weather in France we were making the correct decision, but our son was not convinced at all. Our first stop was near the city of Alicante. We made the decision to stay at a small campsite there, which was adequate for us. The camp site was full of old people, German and British who were on their holidays, away from their country's harsh climates. The very next day we set off, trying not to rush through this alien country, but, we did feel a real sense of displacement. Our son once again began to sleep hours at a time.

The country has no fantastic beauty in its surroundings like the French landscape, it is a journey very different, of thousands of orange trees, as far as your eye can see. There are small service stations which are full of large lorries and fuel tankers on their journeys who knows where. We journeyed on toward Valencia and then decided to drive off the main toll road and in toward the coastal areas. We tried hard to convince our son that this is where we would find real beauty in Spain. We were wrong. We saw new apartment blocks, large plastic sheeted up greenhouses, and a very barren landscape indeed. We followed a sign for a campsite. The camp site was strange, quirky even. We stayed there two days trying to keep to our small routine. Our son discovered a small caravan that had mobiles hung all around it and like most children with imagination, he decided a witch lived there. He was not happy at all, and one by one, his insecurities began coming back.

We made the decision not to stop again in Spain, until we arrived at a familiar place, the home of my parents. We were sure this would help our son to settle, and we were convinced the weather would be better. As we arrived in the Costa del Sol, the weather was a lot nicer, everything looks better when the sun shines. Our son loved his grandparents and could not wait to see them. We still had a long drive after reaching the south of Spain, as my parents lived close to Mabella. When we reached Torremolinos my husband had the idea of driving on the coast road so that we could see the sights. This was also a mistake. At night, or should I say in the dark, everything looks scary and different. This is of course a busy tourist area, and we were in a large motor home, which felt far to big for the roads we were on. In Spain everything comes alive at night, shops are still open, people are going out for tea at ten at night, and everything is busy. The very short drive from Torremolinos to my parents house should have taken one hour, but took us three hours. Just as we were beginning to feel desperation setting in we came upon the familiar sight of my parents home town. We parked up on the promenade, and rang my parents from our mobile telephone. As luck would have it some friends of my parents were visiting them, they had a car, and offered to show us the way to some campsites. So we followed their car to the nearest two campsites both of which did not take dogs. They knew of another site in Marbella, so we followed them to that site and luckily for us they took dogs. The receptionist also spoke some English, so we booked for one night only, in the hope we could have a look around in the light of day, at this time we would decide if we would stay. I admit that our son was beside himself, so after a meal we settled to read our night time story and go to bed, both of us praying everything would look better in the morning.

When we awoke, the sun was shining and the motorhome was warm from the suns rays. We had a slow breakfast outside at our table and chairs, but our son was unhappy about exiting the vehicle. We did not pressure him too, but stated, we were going to walk around the site and we felt he should come to, he declined. My husband and I and Dino walked around this vast site, it was lovely, we were very pleased indeed. We were sure that this campsite was the best we had ever stayed at. The setting was beautiful with trees of every kind, lovely paths and two small restaurants and a small shop. Lots of facilities were available, spread around the site. It had an open air swimming pool and a covered heated one. It also had several children's play areas, one of which was like an outward bounds course for teenagers. We thought this would be an added bonus. We strolled to the reception area and booked into the site for one month, our thoughts were that this area of Spain would have the very best winter weather of all, which we were sure was what we all needed. We were asked to find a plot further inside the campsite, so we climbed back into our vehicle and drove up the winding road, until we found a large grassy pitch in the sun. We set up our table and chairs and simply faced the sun and drank in its warmth. My husband more than any of us needed this warm climate, he had been starved of daylight during his many years working nights. He also needed the time to relax. Our son was unhappy, he would poke his nose out of the motorhome and then retreat back inside. He was a little unhappy we were enjoying the climate so much. We did not argue with him, after all, the question was, how long could he stay inside for ?.

The receptionist had given us leaflets about our surroundings, and they showed that a simple five minute walk away was a small marina. Also five minutes in the opposite direction, was a place of natural beauty, which boasted long beaches. We were sure this information would aid us, in our bid, to get our son outside. We told him he was unable to stay alone in the campsite, it was against the law, (a slight lie of course). So we all set off to explore the marina. Our son seemed to relax before our eyes, he enjoyed looking at the boats and beach bars, he also liked the natural part of the beach which had an ancient tower from the days of the Moors. That evening, we planned to leave Dino in the motorhome, and take the bus to visit my parents. Our son was delighted. This was actually the first time, in my sons life, he had ever been on a bus, we did not realise, but living in the countryside we drove everywhere in a car. Later that evening we called at my parents apartment, and lots of hugs and kisses later, our son began to relax. He chatted happily to his grandparents about his adventures, as my husband and I exchanged a small smile. We went out to a restaurant for tea and we all began to relax further. It was a very nice feeling knowing we were going to be there for at least a month. There was no rush to catch up, as we had all the time in the world. Later that evening we took a taxi back to our campsite and after a short walk we settled for our evening story time.

It never ceases to amaze me how quickly you can begin to enjoy your new surroundings and climate. Every day became similar to before, as we slipped with ease into our routine, of walks and exploring with frequent visits to my parents apartment. We had many meals together and we found out more and more about the area. Our son relaxed at these times, but, on the other hand, he had difficulty adjusting to the campsite life. One day after we had been there three weeks we asked him to call at the reception area and obtain a token for the washing machines. He refused point blank. When our month ended, the new year was upon us and we again decided it would be too cold anywhere else, so we extended our booking for another month. During this second month, our son was asked every other day to go to the reception area and ask for a token for the washing machines and every time he would refuse. If we tried to insist, he would go inside and refuse to come out, or he would shout at us, very loudly.

Many people stay on these sites, many have full time homes there in the form of static caravans, some are on short holidays and others on longer winter sun holidays. There were several family's who had children of all ages. They lived there full time and went to school in the local towns. One evening, around tea time two of these children, girls in fact, called at our pitch and asked my husband and I if we were the parents of the new blond haired boy. We said "yes". They then stated that it was the birthday of one of the girls and that they were having a birthday party, other children from the site would be there, and, they would like to invite our son. We were very happy, our son had never been invited to a birthday party before, and especially not by girls. They did say other boys would be there. We said thank you, that we would ask our son. Of course nothing we said actually persuaded our son to go to this party, he was very cross we had even talked to the girls. He did not go to the party, we were sure this would be his reaction, it saddened us a little. The determination of the young people was lovely. They called at our motorhome daily, requesting that our son go to the park with them or play in the pool with them. Each time he refused to come outside. Just as we were about to despair, one of the older boys on the site rode past our pitch on his mountain bike. He rode backwards and forwards as if to catch our sons attention. When he saw our son he called to him and asked if he would like to get his bike and ride around the site with him. To our absolute shock, our son said he would. Five minutes later we stood open mouthed as our son rode away with the boy.

Over the next few weeks our son began a friendship with this small group of children that would span years. Each child was either from a different country or from a different area. They were of all age groups and they all enjoyed each others company. Our son would happily go off riding, swimming, helping with homework, everything a normal (that word again) child would have done. This was for him his first real friends, and amongst this small group he learnt his first real social skill lessons. How to listen to others, how to laugh at jokes and how to maintain friendships. On some occasions he would even ask for a specific T shirt, which we knew was a choice, he had made, by himself, in a bid to look his best. We look back at this time with a happy heart, because we knew this was progress indeed. Some weeks later, on being asked the same old question regarding a token for the washing machines, our son shocked us rigid by saying "OK", and cycling off in the direction of the reception. When he returned clutching a token, we quietly thanked him and off he went again on his bike, in the direction of his friends. That evening my husband and I celebrated with a bottle of champagne and the next morning my husband extended our stay yet again.

GROWING TOGETHER.

My personal observations of the children in Spain, is that they are younger in themselves, than our children in Britain. This is also true of the children in Germany, where I spent a great deal of my own childhood, even attending school there. Why... ? I am not exactly sure, is it because the adults in these countries celebrate children and youth ?. In Britain we are obsessed with our children growing up quickly, from the clothes the children wear, the gadgets we buy them, to the way we treat them and to the way we expect them to behave. The schools in Britain push the children to perform exact tasks by exact ages. The school system in Spain I believe could teach the Btitish system a thing or two. The system in Spain is in no way perfect but, the children who do not perform certain tasks are simply held back a year. That year is repeated and the child moves forward only when he or she can perform those tasks well. In Spain this is common practice and being held back to repeat certain years carries no stigma at all. It is seen as necessary, especially in this day and age of different nationalities living in each others countries. This gives a child with a language barrier time to catch up. Extra after school classes are given on any subject a child may have difficulty with. The schools in Spain have children of all ages in every year of school life, this gives a more balanced view of society to children.

It was because the children, in themselves, are a little younger here in Spain, and because all the children here are far more accepting of others, that our son was able to forge new relationships, he had never had the opportunity to forge before. At no time did these children in his small group of friends question our sons abilities or the fact he had a slight tremor which grows more pronounced when he feels he is under pressure. They never questioned the fact that he walks a little odd. They simply accepted him as he was. With this acceptance from them and time, we were able to watch our son grow before our eyes. He grew quickly in many ways. He forgot about his panic attacks, he was willing to try new things, he became far more relaxed with others and with himself. He used to say bad phrases about himself like..; I hate myself, I am a horrible person, everyone hates me, I will never have friends, my life is over, I am thick, they think I am thick and stupid, I will never be able to do it, I am useless. These phrases were a daily occurrence from him, as far back in his life as I can remember. Now he began to use phrases like....; hey did you know I have friends, I like the nice weather every day, did you see me riding my bike I am getting quite good at it, I was talking to the couple over there today I actually think they quite like me. These positive phrases, from our son, gave us as parents happier hearts than we had had for years. We thanked god for these moments.

One of the boys was a little naughty, according to his parents and other adults on the site, he also smoked even though he was younger than our son by three years. My son told me that he could not be his friend because of this. I explained to him that this was not the correct approach, that maybe just like him, this boy needed someone to think of him in a better light and maybe he was naughty because this is exactly what others expected of him. I simply asked my son to be more adult about the matter and to think more outside the box than the normal (that word again) people.

The very next day our son brought this young man to our motorhome, he had invited him to tea. He explained to us and his new friend that he had asked the friend not to smoke any more, he continued to say that if he did this he would always be his very good friend. He would help him with his parents and with his school work. This young man did stop smoking that day and he and our son became firm friends. He came to our home as often as possible to eat with us, watch films with us or simply to be. Many months later this friend returned to the UK with his family and years later he still visits our home in Spain. They are fantastic friends and call each other brothers. We are very proud of both boys. What they have overcome and what they have made of themselves.

All the children in this small group developed a sense of freedom as they were allowed by their various parents to take bike rides first around the campsite and then later around a nearby golf course. Our sons ability on a bike grew and grew. He became stronger and developed a sense of achievement in himself. He also had one or two accidents, breaking his collarbone on one occasion and breaking some ribs on another. He broke fingers and had many scrapes and scuffs. However none of this ever deterred him from climbing back on the bike. On some occasions when he simply needed to rest rather than cycle he would say how depressed he was becoming and beg us to allow him to ride his bike again. Even this we saw as positive as he was becoming more aware of his own feelings and how he could help to change those feelings himself.

As a couple we never ever went out. In England we had never gone out, we had always needed to be at home, on hand for our son. When our eldest son grew up he was very mature and responsible, however it seemed wrong to expect him to have the responsibility of looking after our youngest. Going out anywhere was always a family affair. However as our son relaxed into his surroundings in Spain we were able to go to the small bar that was situated on the site and enjoy a bottle of wine, not only did we enjoy this very much ourselves, but we knew it was a right of passage for our son. To allow him to know that we trusted him as a young adult alone and with his friends whilst we were out was very important to him. The trust we placed in him allowed him to grow even further.

At this small site bar, one evening every week they had a quiz night. At first our son would not like to enter the bar, because he hated small crowds of people, smells and noise. On one quiz night he was outside having a drink with his friends when he heard a small group of older people declare that they did not know the answer to the current question. He walked calmly to the table and whispered the answer to them. Our son actually helped the group with many of their questions and to their amusement, they got all the questions right and won the quiz. They asked our son if he would be available the week after and he replied very matter of factly, "I am sorry I do not know my plans for next week, I will help you if I am here". My husband and I simply looked on amused. Word spread quite quickly around the site, of the young man who had helped with the quiz answers. The following week people actually walked out to our son and asked him all manor of questions. He always answered promptly with a small amount of amusement, and, they all got those questions correct.

Again my husband and I smiled quietly to ourselves, as we watched our son with pride. He himself was a little bemused, as he realised, for the first time in his own life, just how clever he was, and, how other adults as opposed to teachers, thought this was fantastic. This evening for our son became a regular event, the quiz master even attempting to find harder and harder questions, trying to catch our son out. He never did. Then the quiz master asked us if we would like to enter the quiz and perhaps we could have our son in our group. We did say it was not really our thing, but he insisted it would help him. So the following week the three of us sat at a table and entered the quiz, of course we won. We did this quiz night for two weeks then my husband declared he did not like quiz nights and that we should be fair to others by not entering again. Our son agreed and declared it was quite boring for him anyway, he would rather be with his friends. Our son then gave back the two prizes we had won from each week, to the quiz master. He never helped again with any answers but he had become famous on the site as the young man who knew everything. He was very humble and yet proud of this, as he walked around the site most of the people shouted hello to him. Because of this, our son began to grow proud of himself rather than seeing his intelligence as a curse.

FAMILY AND BOATS.

The months seemed to roll quickly on and my husband thought this was a time we should look forward and think carefully about our future plans. Our sons improvements were incredible, more than we could ever have dreamed for. However he was correct, we could not live our entire life cocooned in a campsite. It was very difficult even contemplating any move of any kind, for fear of upsetting our new found status quo. During one of our visits to my parents town we called to view the local marina, my husband was very keen for us to be near my parents, but, we were aware our meagre funds would not stretch to any kind of property. Spanish property is very expensive indeed. He began to look at the boats in the small marina and, he came up with the idea of buying a yacht that could be used as a live aboard. It became very plain that even this was almost impossible for us to afford, as all the yachts we could see were very expensive. My husband stepped inside the brokers office and asked to view several of the yachts. As we viewed first one then the other, it became obvious to both of us that they were far to small for us. Our son was growing fast and he was very tall indeed, most of the yachts he would not have been able to stand up in. Actually most of the second bedrooms were very small, having beds in them that were inadequately small for such a growing young man. As we returned to the brokers office, we busied ourselves by looking at the pictures of the yachts on his display board. On the floor, was a picture of a yacht, my husband pointed to it. He asked, "excuse me, is this yacht for sale." The broker said "it was, but he thought it unsuitable for us". My husband asked "why ?", and the broker replied " this yacht has many problems, I think it is a large a project for someone else". My husband immediately asked to see the yacht.

When we walked toward the yacht, I could see my husbands wide smile, I knew that he already wanted this yacht. I on the other hand would be a little harder to convince. When the gangplank was lowered, we walked on board. The yacht had what we lacked at this time in our motorhome, it had space and lots of it. It was huge, and both of us were very capable of turning a project into something worth having. My husband began to make notes, the broker actually got tired of being with us, and so he left us alone for a while. However my husband was tireless in his note making, he looked thoroughly at everything. Much later that day we returned to the campsite. That evening my husband called a family meeting, and the three of us sat down and debated whether we should even attempt to purchase a yacht. He asked us our thoughts and wanted to know if we believed we could live on board a boat. We devised a forward plan whereby my husband would make a long list of the boats problems, and then a list of how much these problems would cost to repair. We would then return to the brokers office the next day and make a very cheap offer armed with our lists. He came up with a figure which was well within our small budget, but he was aware that the broker and seller would not like his offer.

The following day we returned with our son to the marina, my husband made the small offer to the open mouthed broker. As the broker started to refuse, my husband advised the broker that it was a very good offer indeed considering the costs of all the works needed, and he added that if he got this sale for us, he would pay his brokers fee. Smiling, the broker said he would be in touch. My husband told the broker we were leaving the country and going to France on a forward date, he stated, he wished to hear regarding the offer, before this date, or the offer would be withdrawn. On the morning of the day, we were supposedly leaving for France, the telephone rang, and it was the broker, who stated that the offer had been accepted. My husband and son travelled to the marina, papers were signed, monies transferred and one day later we were the proud owners of a fifteen meter, iroko, motor yacht.

It was decided that we would stay a while longer on the campsite and travel daily by bus to the marina. Once there we would begin some of the work needed. The first job was to literally take apart everything in every room, the seating, the beds, wardrobes, kitchen and bathrooms.

The deck of the yacht had been leaking for many years and because it had never been repaired, everything was spoilt from rain water. My husband and son worked very hard. My husband gave out instructions and my son endeavoured to follow them. It warmed my heart to see them working so closely together, I realised how lucky we were, as most family's never get such an opportunity.

At the beginning our son seemed not to be affected from the current change of events, this was a first. However looking back to this time, I now realise that he simply had not realised that us owning a yacht would inevitably mean we would move from the campsite. The actual day of moving off the campsite came quicker than we had originally planned. The simple journey back and forth on the bus was in itself tiring, and it also meant that we lost hours of good work time each day. If we were located at the marina, we could work inside much later in the evening, and also start earlier in a morning. My husband did a deal with the owner of the car park which was located at the port entrance. This deal would mean we could park our motor home there full time and be on hand to work longer hours. We felt sad for our son, this change would mean he would not be able to hang out with his friends every evening, but we knew we needed to make the change.

When we moved to the marina our son was affected a little. He began to sleep long hours through the day, on the front deck, in a deck chair. We would make small jokes about how being on the water rocked him to sleep, but it was a development had become quite used to. We knew that he simply needed time to adjust. When he did work with my husband, he worked very hard. As he has got a little older he has developed a good sense of humour. He would tell jokes or he would do impressions of certain actors or people he had met. His love of cars had grown almost to an obsession and he would talk endlessly about the cars he and his father would some day build together. He continued to ride his bike daily around the new town but it seemed almost impossible for him to meet new friends. The towns location makes it fantastic for old people who want either to retire to the sun, or simply have extended holidays. Young people therefore are much harder to find. My parents lived in close proximity to the marina which meant family life was a little fuller, this also meant our son could independently visit his grandparents.

A few weeks later it became clear that the work we could achieve whilst the boat was in the water was coming to an end, we needed to lift the boat into a dry dock facility to do the rest. However this brought about new problems we had failed to realise before. Our yacht was far to large and heavy for the dry dock facility in our location. The crane their was only a small one, the nearest dry dock that had a larger crane was a five and a half hour boat journey up the coast. My husband had also to take an exam which is required by Spanish law prior to taking a yacht anywhere. With our yacht booked into the new dry dock facility and my husbands exam in place, a date was set for our new relocation. It was determined that I would take our belongings up the coast by road and my husband, son and Dino would go by sea.

During the journey my husband spent most of his time checking and re checking the engines, whilst our son drove the boat. My husband reported how calm our son was and how grown up he had behaved. My husband felt that his ability to drive a fifteen meter motor yacht without any prior experience was fantastic. Both journeys by road and by sea went without any hitch. Our yacht was lifted into a large yard area and our motor home was parked outside the gates. The very next day work on the yacht began but the sheer size of our new project had only just begun to sink in. She was absolutely huge out of the water and we now realised that the few weeks we had originally set aside for the project would need extending.

In total we were in our new location for exactly one year, during this year we all worked together. There were times when this was simply too much for our son and on these occasions we simply allowed him to be. At the end of the year my son drove the motor yacht back to our port of origin with my husband closely checking and re checking the engines, I drove the motor home as before.

When we arrived back in our berth we decided that we should move into the yacht as the motor home seemed simply far to small. We also decided that we should sell the motor home as two homes were too much for anyone. We were all very happy to be back home, we missed the area more than we thought we would. We had missed my parents also and it felt good for us all to be together again.

A few days later we received terrible news, my father had become ill and he had been to see a doctor. He had left the doctors surgery with a list of medication needed, that was similar in length, to a housewife's shopping list. We quickly realised that, he was in fact, much sicker than he was telling us. A few weeks later my father was taken to hospital very ill, he was in intensive care and later that day he slipped into a coma. He was actually in the coma for several weeks and we were advised by the medical staff that he may not pull through. This news was devastating for us all, but for our sons, it seemed catastrophic. Our sons love of their grandparents is immense. I am sure that is true for most grandchildren but our children's love for for these people, who had always been a part of their lives showed no bounds. Our worry was for my mother who had been with my father for over fifty years, and for all our family, but also for our youngest son who never reacted well to change. How would he react to this dreadful news ? Well I can tell you he did not react well at all, he simply refused to accept that he may in any way loose his grandfather. He told me over and over that it would not happen, I should not talk that way, that my father would not leave us, he loved us all too much to die. Our son would not accept that his grandfather may not come home. My father did actually pull through and weeks later we brought him home. However he was a changed man, he was now very weak. He was wheelchair bound and unable to do most tasks he had previously done with ease. He grew increasingly thinner and weaker, I was very glad that we were around to help. Months later, during a meal at their apartment, which my husband had cooked especially for my parents, my father suffered a massive heart attack. He was taken by the paramedics to the hospital and placed on a ventilator. My father died a few days later.

Our youngest son was incredible at this moment, unlike the previous occasion. He cuddled me and simply stated; " mum, I know you are very sad now, you are crying for yourself. Granddad is now in a better place, he no longer hurts, he is happy. Granddad knew this was his time to die and he is at peace. I know this to be true, I have faith."

That was a miraculous moment in my life for many reasons, but mostly because it showed true love, true caring and a wonderful belief. I looked up at this very tall young man who stood at my side and for the first time I realised just how much he had grown into a wonderful human being.

The new problem came for us all when my son started having terrible nightmares with regard to my mothers health and safety. He now knew first hand that his grandparents were not always going to be around, they simply would not live forever. He could not shake his thoughts and he was not willing to contemplate loosing his grandmother. This thought terrified him. He requested that he be allowed to move into my parents apartment so that he could simply be near her. He somehow thought that by being there he would prevent anything bad happening. My mother agreed, and a day later my son moved from the yacht into their apartment. Our youngest son stayed with my mother for many months, only willing to move out when his older brother came home. The idea was that his brother could now take his place and keep my mother safe. I am sure their grandma did not realise that she would be unable to get rid of our sons as they took it upon themselves to decide what was best for her.

When our middle son left Spain for his new employment we persuaded our youngest that his grandma was quite capable of looking after herself now. He did not like this news, but he accepted it anyway. Today he is a very frequent visitor to her home.

TOE BY TOE IN A BRAVE NEW WORLD.

When we arrived back to our own mooring, in the marina that was to become our new home, we felt far more relaxed, than we had done before. Having moved onto the yacht we could all spread out in our new larger space, our son had a bedroom all to himself, with a new bed which was two meters long. This for him was luxurious, being so tall was very inconvenient when it came to getting a good nights sleep. Having his own space, was important to him, a space he could personalise once again.

For the first time in a long time we all felt very much at home, but we were changed people. We had learnt that home is very much where your heart is, and that with a little effort we could live a good life in another country. We were all very much more relaxed as individuals, our son would chuckle when he saw the British tourists, never fully relaxed from their stressful lives in Britain.

As regards education for our son, we were unsure, at this point, in which direction to go, we thought long and hard about the situation. Of course we still wanted him to progress and he was progressing. As an individual he was far more confident, he had some faith in his own abilities. How could we expand on this ? That was the question we mulled over for quite a while.

My husband had made a friend on the port, this man had a boat, which was used in the summer months to run trips for the tourists.

In a conversation one day he told my husband how many of the beach businesses struggled each year to find staff to work on the beach. The reason for this, was that the Spanish government required all the staff within these businesses to have a special qualification. This qualification was an adopted American marine course. The thinking behind this, was that all the staff were trained in all aspects of boat and sea safety. It seemed very reasonable to me that they should require this qualification. After my husband related this conversation to me I began thinking. A short burst of employment would give us, as our sons parents, an indication as to whether he could cope with a work situation or not. Of course first he would have to pass the qualification. We had observed him during our last twelve months further up the coast and he seemed to have a natural ability when it came to the sea.

The first course we booked him on was the the British SSR, power boat level 2. This course was run over two days, it follows simple survival at sea, boat safety, and a day driving and parking a boat. I first went to the gentleman who ran these courses and explained that our son was very dyslexic, but very intelligent. I explained to him that if he would give me a book with the course details in, I could read this to our son first. Then I was more secure in the knowledge he would have the greatest success. This is exactly what we did, and our son one week later was the proud owner of his first exam qualification since we set off from England.

I trawled the internet and made several phone calls and was able to book our son onto a course in our local town. This course is an American marine course. It was to be taken entirely in Spanish over the course of a week. (Our son did not speak Spanish at this time, although he knew many individual words). Five very long days, with an exam at the end. The course is also very costly indeed. Sending our son off every day was very hard indeed for us as parents. He found the course difficult to follow and at times very boring. Our instructions to him were simply to watch and listen and learn. To our utter amazement our son passed the exam and was the proud owner of his new Spanish qualification.

We were more proud of our son than you can imagine and more importantly he was proud of himself. My husband and I saw this as an absolute triumph. This convinced us that we were correct to bring him away from England. He had the opportunity to be successful, an opportunity he would not have got in the UK. I took these qualifications to a gentleman who owned one of these beach businesses. I explained our son was looking for work for the summer holidays , if he needed staff. He said he was looking for staff and he set up a meeting with our son. The result of this informal meeting was that our son was offered a job for the first time in his life.

In this beach business they had a para sail boat and they offered banana rides and ringo rides and of course they had many of the inevitable small pedal boats we all love during our holidays by the sea.

Exactly what his job would entail we did not know at this point, but he had a job, that was all that mattered to us. Another success.

We had no idea if our son could manage this job or not, because it is long hours of work, in blistering heat. He would also need to work within a small team and we did not know if he would be able to do this. To some people on a two week holiday this job would appear to be idyllic but I can tell you that it is very hard work indeed, for not very much money.

We agreed with our son that, with his wages he could purchase a new computer, a special one that he had coverted for some time. After this purchase, we asked that all his wages be saved and used for education in the winter months, he agreed.

Work was very hard for him, as I am sure it is for any youngster during their very first real job. He was very good at his job, he was more intelligent than most of the other workers there and as usual this did present some problems. However, our son did work very hard, in forty degrees of heat, with a small team of men, for very long hours. At the end of the day he was exhausted, often sleeping as soon as he arrived home, even refusing his evening meal. The pride we felt was immeasurable, the joy for him, for his success was better than winning the lottery.

Our son did purchase his new computer, with his first very hard earned wage. The beach business even asked him to work for them the following year. The real question for us now was, what education could he do during the winter months ?. Learning the language was a must for us all, but our son found it very difficult, as did we. I purchased some language tapes and we only had Spanish TV, but still at this time it seemed too difficult a task.

On a walk through the port I came up with my new idea for education. There was a small Spanish business just opening nearby. This was a Spanish diving school. I thought it was a similar theme so I called in to speak to the owner. I advised him that our son needed a new hobby, and I couldn't think of better a hobby than one where you could actually gain qualifications. The business was a new one and he needed customers, it seemed perfect. I did tell the owner of our sons dyslexia, but he assured me there would be no problems. They used video footage as well as books. The first two day small course in diving was booked for the following week.

Some times in your life you experience something that feels as if all your Christmases have come at once. This is how we felt as parents when our son was taken on his first diving course. He absolutely loved it, and I mean loved it. He talked about nothing else, all talk of cars was suddenly gone. He stayed with the diving school, doing many qualifications even his specialist deep open water dive and his dive master. He simply adored being in the water and seeing the beauty that hid beneath. He purchased all his own diving gear and underwater cameras. He even looked on the internet at the possibility of attending another school, in America or Australia, with a view to having a career in diving. These schools were unavailable to a person with no money from the UK, but whatever happens in our sons future he has these qualifications and he has had the experience. This period in our sons life was simply positive.

Our sons second year working for the beach business went a little better than the first. He was a little more used to the others who also worked there. He knew what was expected during the working days and was more adjusted to the high temperatures and longer working hours. He was also given the job of driving the rescue boat. This means he works alone for most of the day at sea, taking people backwards and forwards to the various activity's. He also collects any people who fall into the sea. He was meeting holiday makers of all nationalities daily, and he was also meeting the Spanish locals who lived nearby. Even the Guardia who's job it is to patrol the sea really, like our son. I preen myself often and say, " well what's not to like". Of course it is not my hard work or my husbands , it is due to the hard work of our son.

After the death of my father, my mother gave all the grandchildren a sum of money. She told them that it was their granddad's wishes that they have this money. Our youngest son decided to buy a bicycle with his money. However it was not just any old bike, he chose a custom made frame which I ordered for him on the internet. He spent hour after hour sourcing parts for this bike, brakes, forks, seat. He obtained parts from all over the world. This bike is beautiful, he built it with my husband and afterwards, he started to ride daily. He rode hours at a time and some months later he asked my husband to ride with him.

I did not actually understand very much about bikes , I admit, but I learnt quite fast. My son purchased a special post war folding shovel and trowel. Every day, they would be seen cycling off, to make special down hill bike runs. Nearby is a mountain which has a cable car run to the top. They would ride the cable car, complete with bikes and then ride their bikes downhill. My husband one evening declared that our son was actually very good indeed. Our son decided to enter the Spanish downhill mountain bike championships. This is ridden throughout the year, over several courses, around Spain. They trained lots and I was simply amazed that this was the same young man who struggled to ride a bike for many years. Now he was entering a Spanish tournament. Tents were bought, sleeping bags, and extra tires and inner tubes. My husband took our son all over Spain in order for him to take part in the competition. Unfortunately some of the meetings were during his third year of work, during the busiest weeks of summer. His employer actually gave him three days off for one meeting but would not allow another. (this was unfortunate but understandable)

I can report that our son came fortyfith out of hundreds. We felt like he had won. To have taken part was amazing, to have missed some of the meets were unfortunate, but to have come so far and done so well, for us meant he was a winner.

It was during this time that our sons childhood pet and constant companion, Dino died. His cancer suddenly became unbearable for him, it happened during one of our sons long days at work.

111

I was so sad, as was my husband, this dog had been the most amazing family pet. Telling our son was the hardest thing we had ever had to do. Our son walked down his steps, into his room, he quietly closed his door, and he sobbed for hours. I left him to his own thoughts for a while, but because his sobbing grew stronger, I knocked on his bedroom door. My son was led face down on the floor, devastated. Consoling him was an impossible task, grief is an emotion as parents we all wish we could shield our children from. The next day I informed our sons employer, he had a stomach bug and that he was unable to work. I knew from the past that this would allow our son time to sleep and adjust. The following morning our son rose for his working day, looking very pale and sad. He cuddled me and reminded me how ill Dino had been, he told me not to be sad,he said he was sure his granddad and Dino were together now. He told me how he felt a little happier knowing they had each other. Our son wept for several nights after this event, as did we, as we listened quietly, trying to remember as his parents that his grief was a natural emotion. We did worry about the future, we did not know if he would be able to cope. In the past, an event like this would have taken our son years to adjust to. Our son did cope and he did finish the entire summer season at work, even though emotionally, it had been his most difficult yet.

As I reflect on this period in our sons past I cannot help but feel proud, he has proven, that he can move forward. That he can learn new things and that he can perfect old ones. He has grown not just in height but emotionally. He has weathered sad events and has found the strength within to carry on, even offering his love, strength and kindness to others around him.

THE FUTURE LOOKS BRIGHTER.

Our son has developed a keen interest in fashion over the last two years, this is healthy and normal for a young man of his age. In the past he had no interest in fashion, because he disliked himself so much. His self image was something which preoccupied his thoughts, in a negative way, for many years. At 6ft 8inches tall I watch him today walking down a street, with his head held high, and yes, he still walks in his own dyspraxic way, but our young man is a calm and confident one.

In January 2010, our son met a young girl. This lovely girl was introduced to our son through a friend. She is Spanish and spoke no English, our son is English and spoke very little Spanish. Over the next few months we observed our son trying to speak Spanish with all the strength he could muster. Today in January 2011, our son speaks fluent Spanish.

When my son was young he would ask me if he would ever have a girlfriend, and I would say yes, that somewhere, there was someone for him. He never, ever, believed me. This young lady is 21 years old in March 2011, and is simply a delight. For some reason, having a language barrier to conquer, gave them both the extra time they needed to understand and know each other. This means that when our son is slow getting ready, she giggles with me, but understands. When he is unable to choose, the house is filled with laughter from them both, as they try with difficulty to decide together.

If I had chosen this young lady myself, I could not have chosen better. Through her, our son now has a large group of friends, which are mostly Spanish and some are other nationality's. All his friends accept him for who he is.

Some people get ingrown toenails, our son has an ingrown laptop. He is never without it. On the internet, he has joined a special group. Through this group he helps young people who have eating disorders and who simply need a friend.

He also contributes to a web site in Canada, in this site, many people from all over the world discuss their love of classic cars. A special feature is shown every week which consists of a classic car theme Tuesday, showcasing cars and how they can be modified . This feature is done entirely by our son.

Through his laptop he is in constant contact with his friend, whom he met when we lived in the motor home in Mabella. This young man, our son calls his brother. He stays with us often, travelling the distance from Britain. They talk daily and will be very close friends for life. Our new adopted son, accepts our son for who he is, turning to him for help and guidance. Trusting him no matter what.

This winter our sons choice of education was to obtain a special world wide accepted, commercial boat licence. He gained this licence with relative ease, again building on the skills that come naturally to him.

With this licence he may be able to work a slightly longer summer season. He has also begun learning French, which I am happy to report is going very well. Having one language under his belt has given him the confidence to try another.

As far as dyslexia is concerned Spanish is easier to write, the reason for this is that it is a phonetic language. Put simply, they pronounce all the letters in every word, unlike English that has strange rules a dyslexic person finds hard to understand.

What the future holds for our son , I really do not know. Is our son still Dyspraxic ? The answer is yes. Is our son still Dyslexic ? The answer is also yes. Every day of every year, now and for his future, he will have to work hard in certain areas of his life. This will never go away. He will always worry a little too much and he will always struggle adapting to change. He will never eat with a knife and fork and he will find it very difficult to suffer fools gladly.

Today however our home is filled with laughter, as we all learn to laugh out loud. If we feel sad, we all say so and we cuddle and tell those we love, as often as possible, how important they are to us.

Our son today is a very clever, proud and slightly eccentric individual. He has a deep understanding of other people and listens to them offering his advise where needed. He has several hobbies which as a young boy, he could only have dreamt about. He has more determination than any one I have ever known. It was never possible for our son to shrink into any background, as he was always taller and blonder than any individual around him. He is very striking in his looks and always was. Today he is six feet eight inches tall, slim with the blondest hair you have ever seen. When he walks down a street everyone looks at him. He has had to learn to be proud of who he his, and he has had to learn to hold his head up high. Our entire family marvel at the strong individual he has become today.

My message to any family of a very young child who has dyslexia or dyspraxia is simply this;.....

do not despair. Listen to all the advise you are given. But more than that, listen to your child. Never ever ever give up, and never ever forget that the world is full of billion's and billion's of individuals. That is the key word, INDIVIDUALS, we may like similar fashion as others and we may like similar food, but we are our own person. There is no correct time span for doing anything, it is simply what is right for that individual. EMBRACE BEING YOURSELF.

The last words of advise in this book are my sons;........

He says that his worst problem of all growing up was not that people refused to listen to him or that they always treated him like an idiot. His worst problem amongst his thousands of problems was that he simply could not stop thinking. He could never ever shut off and simply be. It did not matter what he did or where he was, in a classroom, in church, at home, in front of a TV or computer, or even in bed. His thoughts worked over time and would not allow him to concentrate properly on anything. This was his problem at the age of three and it is his problem today. Today however he has learnt to occupy his thoughts with the use of music . When he cycles he listens to soft classical music. When he wakes in a morning he listens to happy upbeat music. He has a vast eclectic taste in music from classical to punk , which he uses to help him throughout his day and night. When he discovered that music could help him he was sixteen years of age. This was around the time that he began to make huge steps forward in his life.